Ga nzio
and the Vittoriale

"Leave me that which is mysterious, fleeting,
and incomprehensible in me."

Gabriele d'Annunzio, *Di me a me stesso*

Anna Villari

Gabriele d'Annunzio and the Vittoriale

Historic and artistic Guide

SilvanaEditoriale

Cover
The Vittoriale, Officina (Workshop)

Silvana Editoriale

Produced by
Arti Grafiche Amilcare Pizzi Spa

Direction
Dario Cimorelli

Art Director
Giacomo Merli

English Copy Editor
Lorena Ansani

Layout
Denise Castelnovo

Translations
Elizabeth Tauroza for *Scriptum*, Rome

Production Coordinator
Michela Bramati

Editorial Assistant
Valentina Miolo

Iconographic office
Deborah D'Ippolito, Mira Mariani

Press office
Lidia Masolini, press@silvanaeditoriale.it

Thanks to

Giordano Bruno Guerri
President of the Fondazione Il Vittoriale degli Italiani

Roberta Valbusa and Alessandro Tonacci
of the Archivio-Biblioteca del Vittoriale for their valuable collaboration

Contents

1. Entrance
2. Piazzetta of the Victory of the Piave
3. Parlaggio
4. Esedra
5. Piazzetta Dalmata
6. Prioria
7. Prioria's Garden
8. Schifamondo
9. Viale di Aligi
10. Dolphin's Fountain
11. MAS
12. Cruiser *Puglia*
13. Acqua Pazza
14. Acqua Savia
15. Lake of Dances
16. Mausoleum

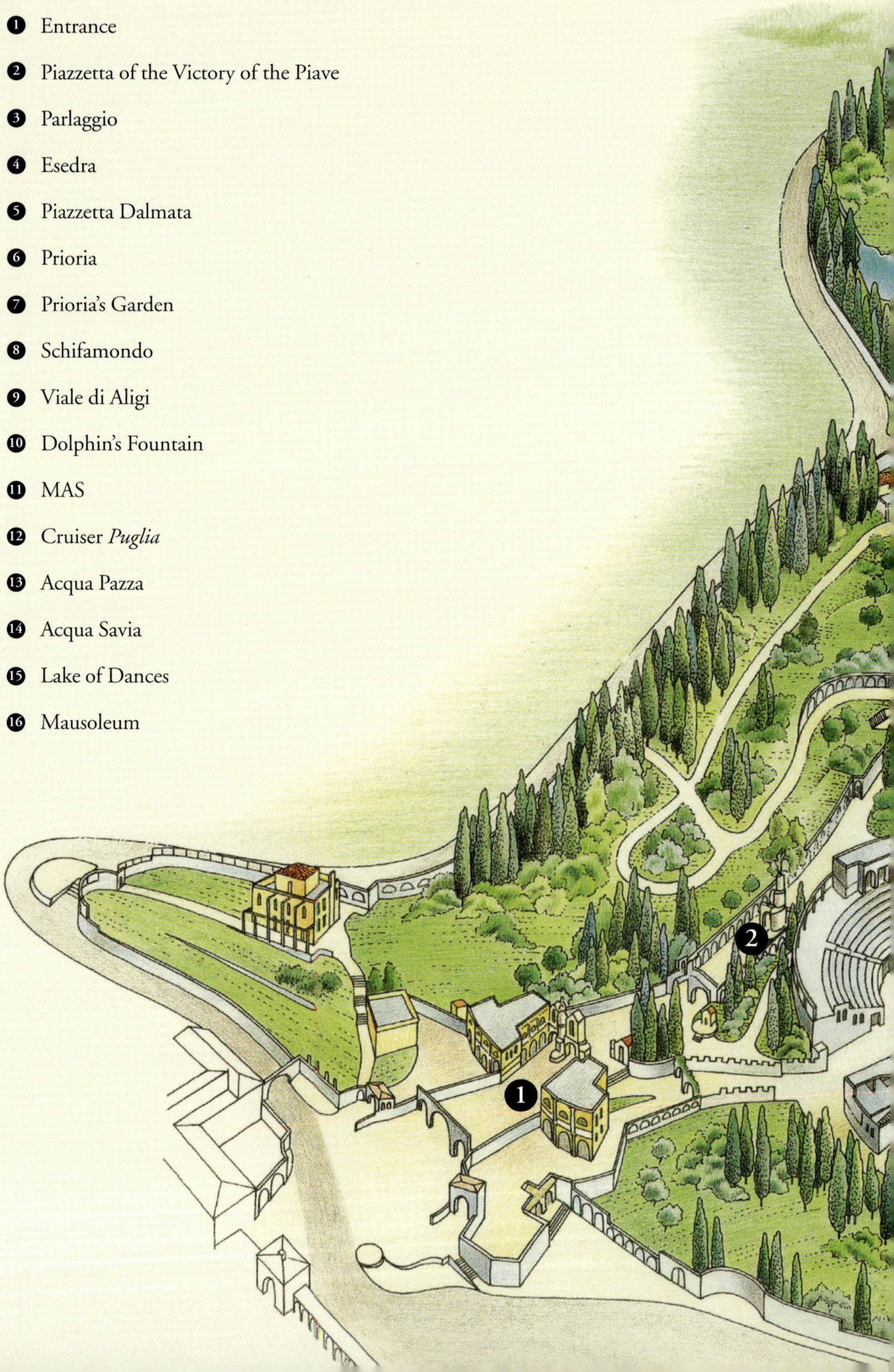

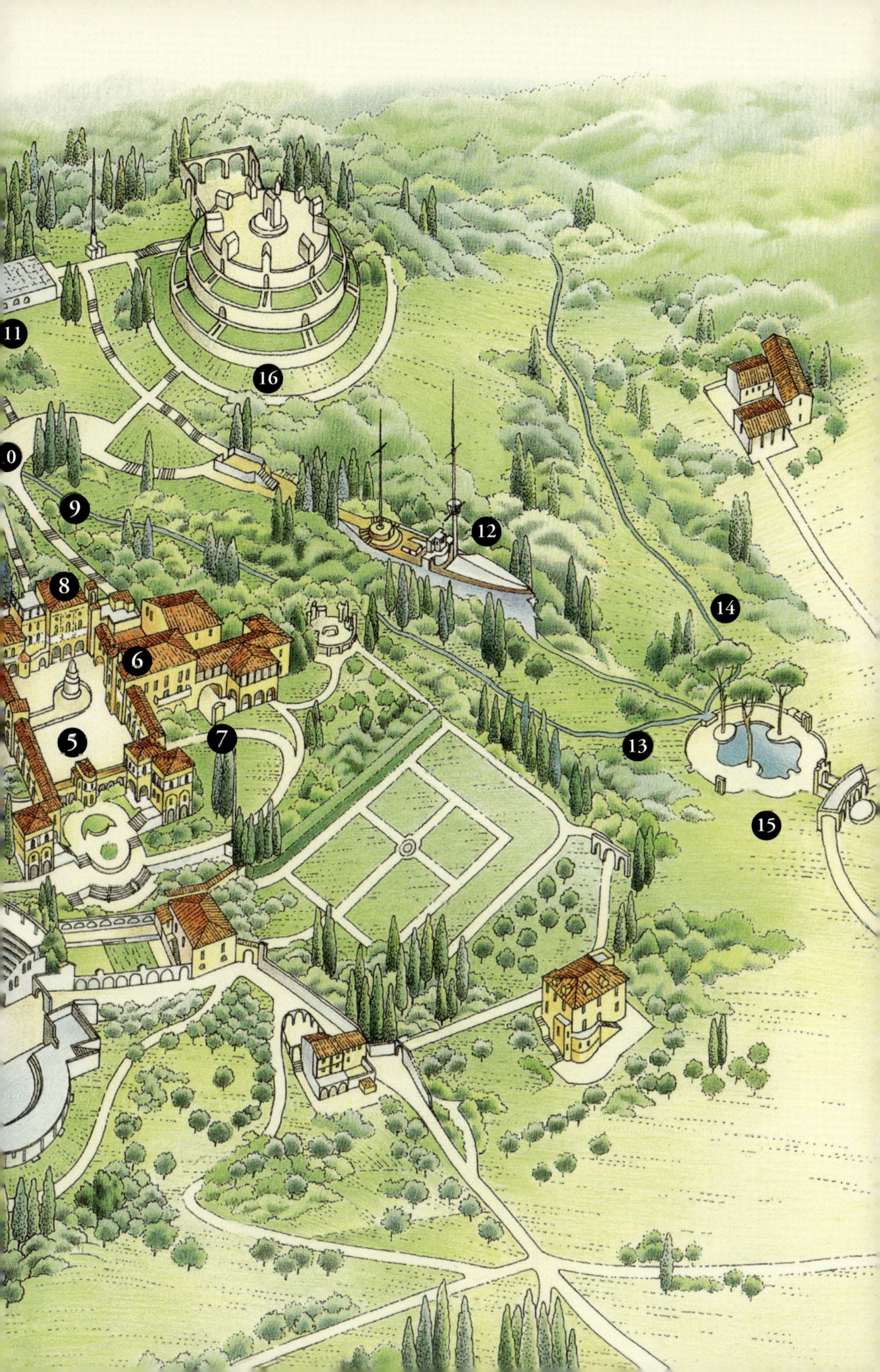
11
16
0
9
12
8
6
14
7
13
5
15

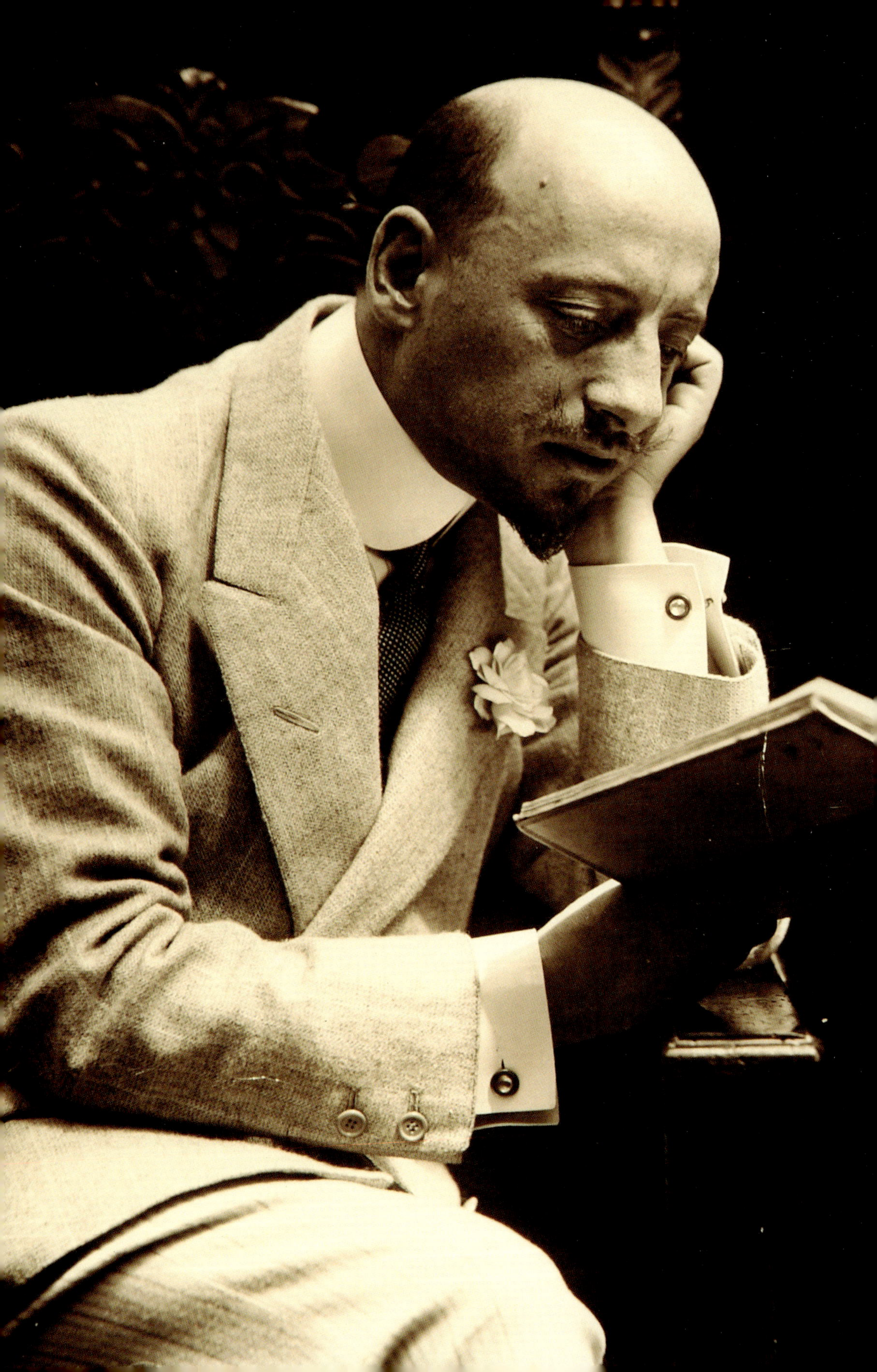

Gabriele d'Annunzio and the Creation of the Vittoriale

As a young ambitious poet, as an acclaimed writer, as an exile in a foreign land, as a politician and commandant, Gabriele d'Annunzio always liked to live in places that matched him, that were transformed into his image and likeness until they became bizarre and sophisticated luxury residences. His novels abound in detailed descriptions of elegant environments full of fine objects, so that we may find an increasingly valid parallel, in literature as in life, between d'Annunzio's tastes and predilections as a man, and his most intimate spiritual and aesthetic disposition.
A "man of luxury", by his own definition, who was never satisfied, from his early youth Gabriele loved things – indeed, he needed them: precious objects, works of art, books, and furniture; in his lyric poem *Canta la gioia* (in *Canto Novo*, published in 1882), written before he had even reached his twenties, he declared to the world his "immense joy at being alive,/ at being strong, young, at eating the fruits of the earth/with strong, white, voracious teeth,/ of putting bold, greedy hands on every tangible object [...]."
On 6 April 1886, the young poet wrote in a letter to Prince Maffeo Sciarra Colonna, owner of "La Tribuna" magazine which d'Annunzio edited during the first few years of his period in Rome: "By temperament and instinct, I feel the need for *superfluous things*. My spirit leads me irresistibly to desire and acquire beautiful things. I could easily have lived in a modest house, sat on Vienna chairs, eaten from common plates, walked on an Italian-made carpet, drunk tea from a cheap cup, blown my nose on Schostal or Longoni handkerchiefs. But instead, fatally, I wanted sofas, precious fabrics, Persian carpets, Japanese plates, bronzes, ivories, knick-knacks, all those useless, beautiful things that I love with a deep, ruinous passion."
It was precisely because of this "ruinous passion", this perpetual desire to buy and accumulate, that d'Annunzio constantly had to flee from the city, from the houses that he loved and had decorated with care, but

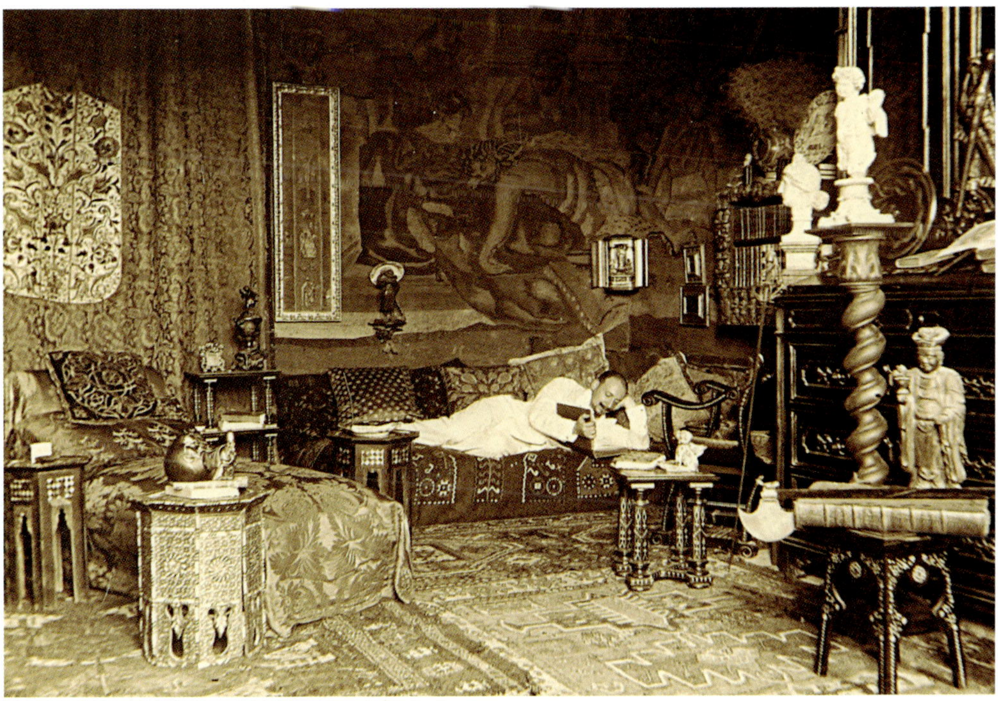

Gabriele d'Annunzio at the Capponcina, in a photo by Mario Nunes Vais

D'Annunzio In the study at the Villa Mammarella in Francavilla del Mare

Eleonora Duse as Francesca da Rimini

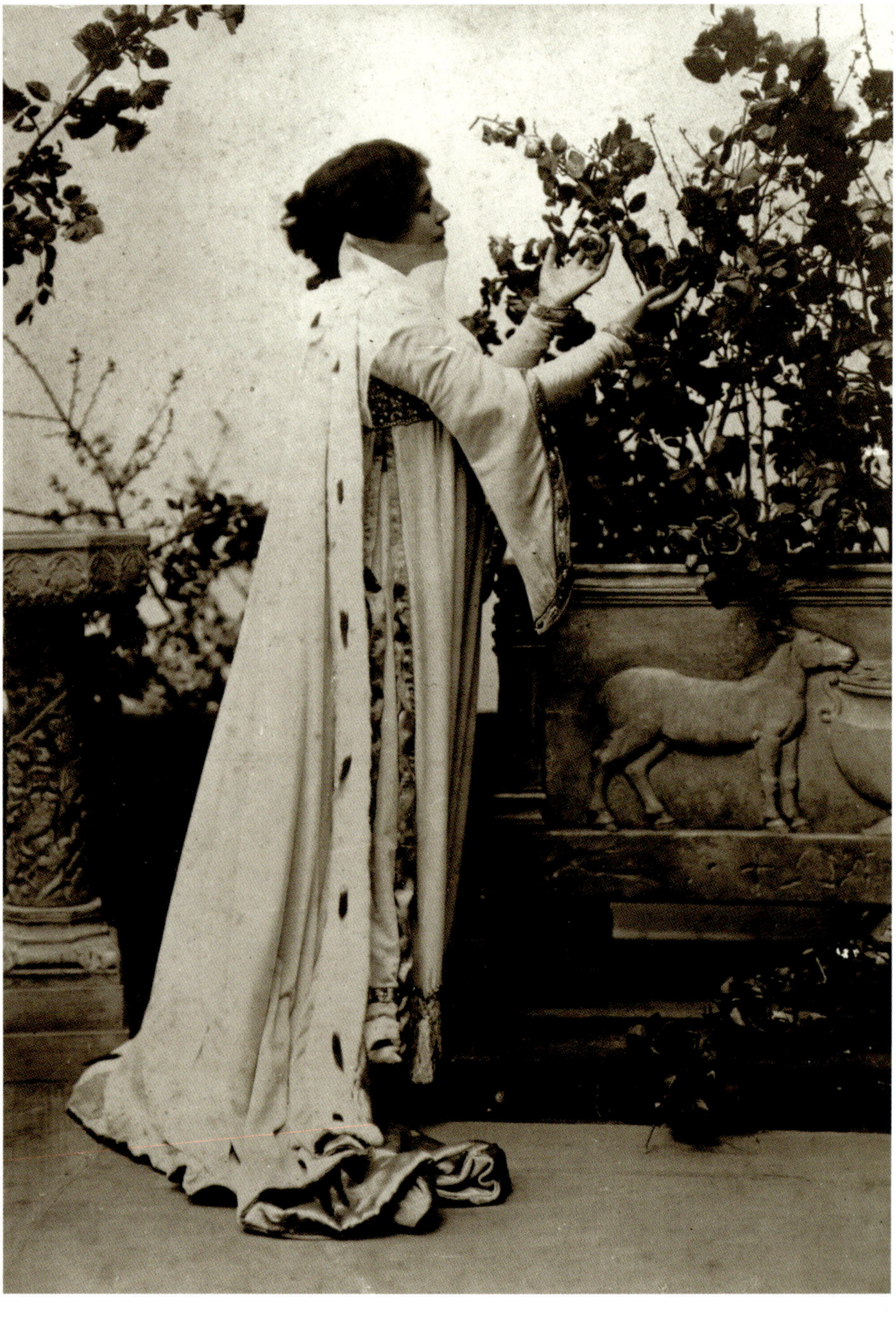

Gabriele
d'Annunzio
on horseback
at La Capponcina

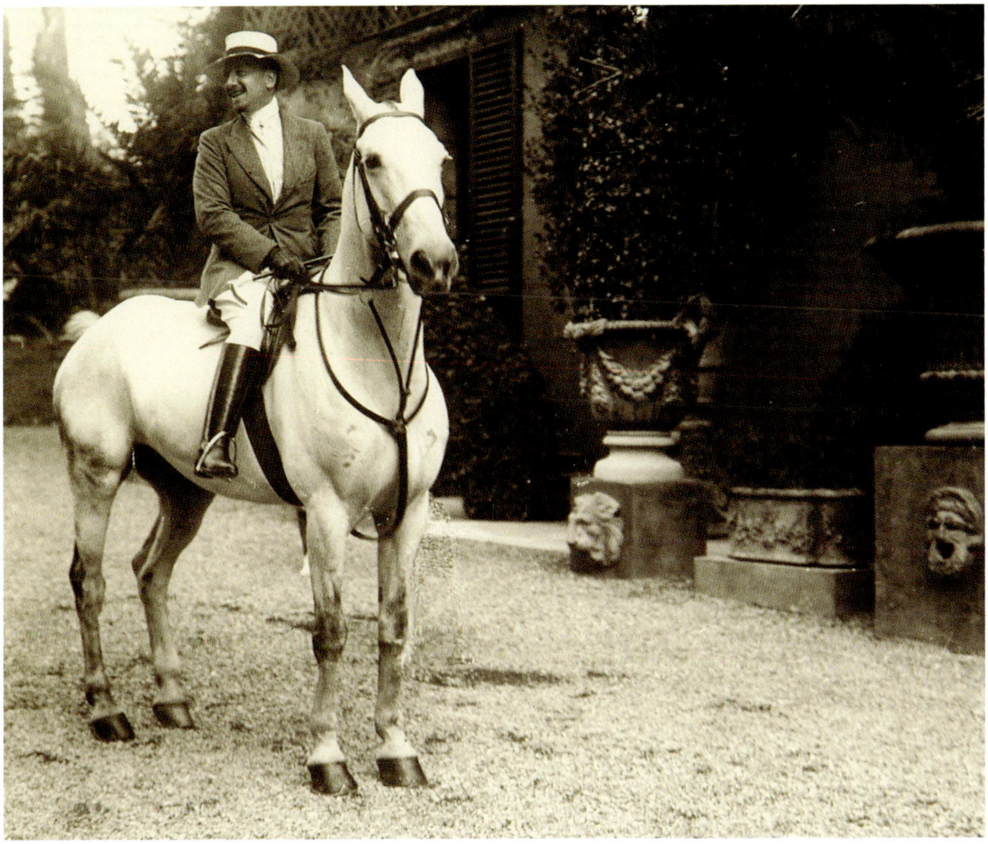

which were too expensive and, in the end, impossible to maintain. As a frequent visitor to museums, a connoisseur of works of art and the skills of the artisan, defender of the nation's "cultural heritage", which was not at that time adequately protected by conservation laws, and with an aesthetic sensibility that was so marked as to border on the pathological, d'Annunzio tended to transform his homes – whether for long or short periods – into treasure troves, places of every kind of delight for the intellect and the body. It was thus with his Rome apartment in Via Gregoriana, evoked in *Piacere*, and in the villa called La Capponcina, on the hills of Settignano, near Florence, from 1898 the scene of an intense and creative love affair with the "divine" Eleonora Duse. "The old Capponi villa, devastated and plundered by the wind of creditors" as Gabriele was to write later, it was wrenched from him, in the true sense of the word, because of the tradesmen and suppliers who were tired of his hopeless debts. Or again, in the chalet of Saint-Dominique in Arcachon, Aquitaine, on the shores of the Atlantic ocean, where he spent part of his French exile (1910-1915) in order to escape from the pressure of his debts, while always yearning for Italy.

"Stained glass windows, curtains, blinds on the doors and windows to keep out sun, noise and prying eyes from rooms in semi-darkness like sanctuaries, and, like them, perfumed with incense and lit with candles and torches [...] rooms as intimate as cells, hung with damask like alcoves, cluttered with missals, lecterns,

Gardone Riviera
in a postcard
from the period

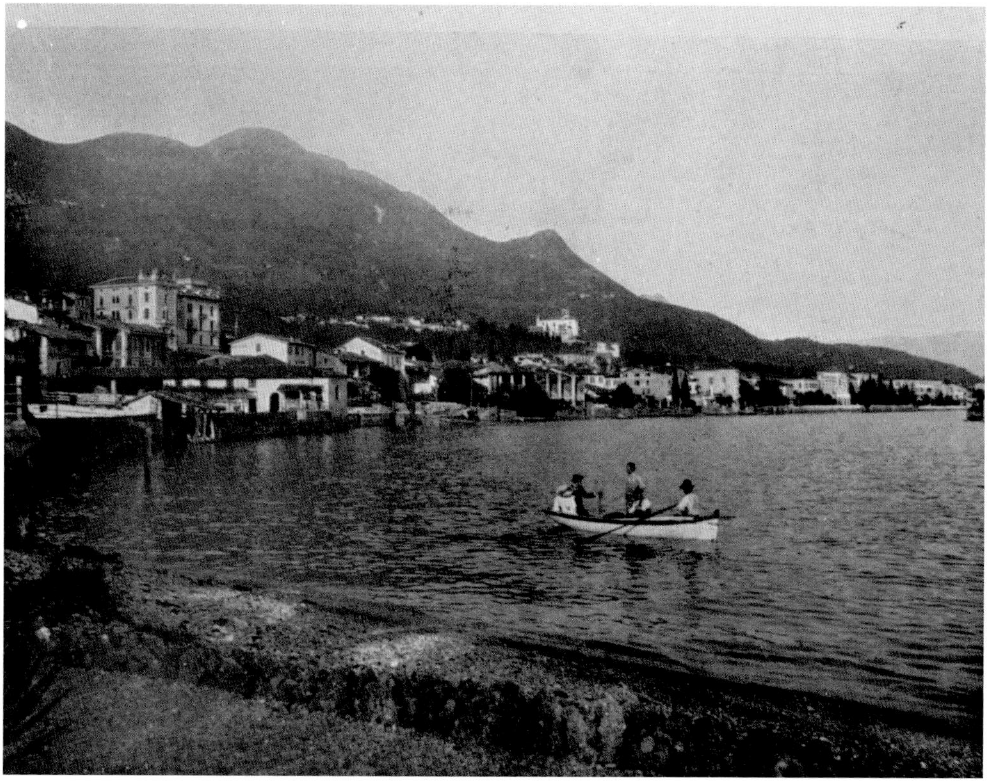

saints, cushions, bells, coats of arms, hour glasses, candelabras, and mottos [...]." This was the mysterious tone with which art critic Ugo Ojetti, a friend and admirer of d'Annunzio, remembered the Settignano villa in 1924 – and photos and stories confirm his evocative description – before almost all the objects, paintings, books and even his beloved horses were seized in July 1909, to be sold at auction in June 1911. It was a continual encumbering, crowding, and filling up of rooms that were kept in semi-darkness in order to make things appear only dimly, and later, as he grew older, to hide himself from view – from himself and from strangers. We read, in another of Ojetti's memoirs written in 1938, how objects, ornaments and knick-knacks were jumbled together at Capponcina "one inside another, like Chinese boxes. A bust on top of a chest; around the neck of the bust a piece of jewellery; on the jewellery, a flower [...]."
We see the same tendency to accumulate, the same dense atmosphere, bewitching and frantic both at the same time, in the rooms of the Vittoriale; but here the whole situation was different from the very beginning: the affection for the place was complete and definitive, and the Villa Cargnacco, on Lake Garda, adapted from an eighteenth century farmhouse, was the only one, out of all of d'Annunzio's many homes, that he bought.
While staying in Venice, on his return from the exhilarating but tiring experience in Fiume – 15 months ruling the city, which had been conquered with arms and turned into an independent Republic with the support of a group of "legionnaires" – d'Annunzio was informed of the villa's availability by his faithful secretary, Tom Antongini, at the end of January 1921. His friends and collaborators had been searching for a suitable place of rest for "the Prophet" and warrior for several months in a lake region in the north of Italy – the

Villa Cargnacco before d'Annunzio's arrival

The gardens of Villa Cargnacco

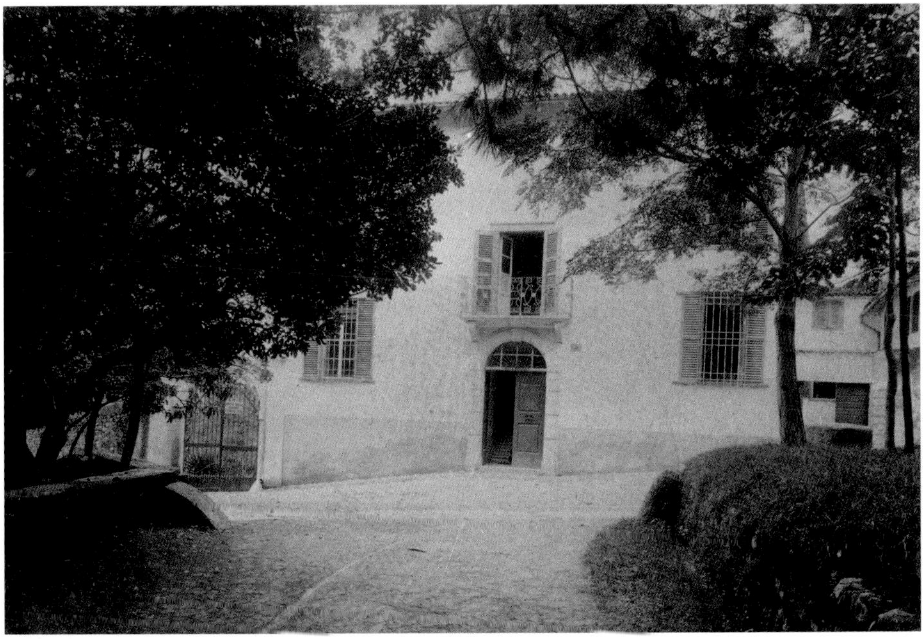

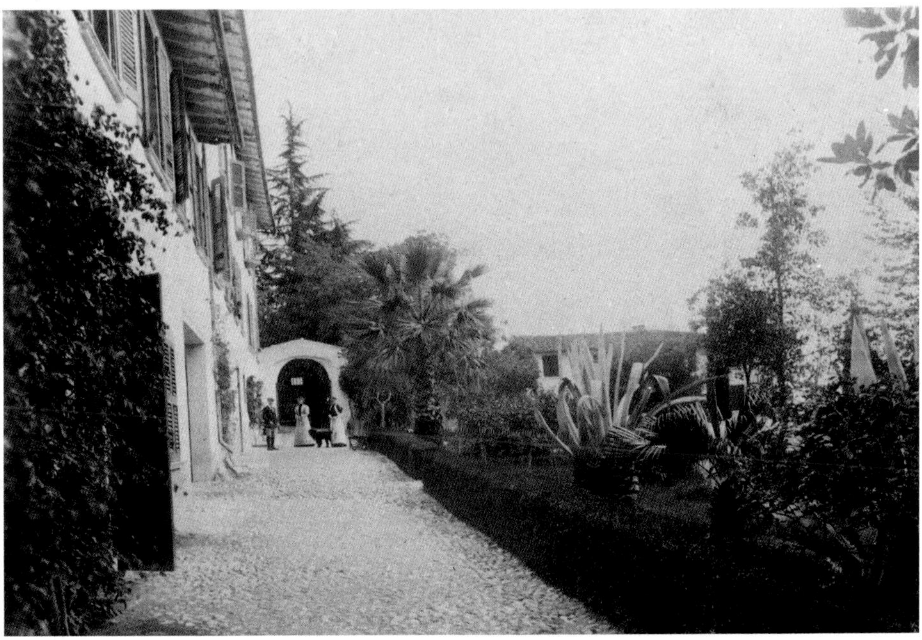

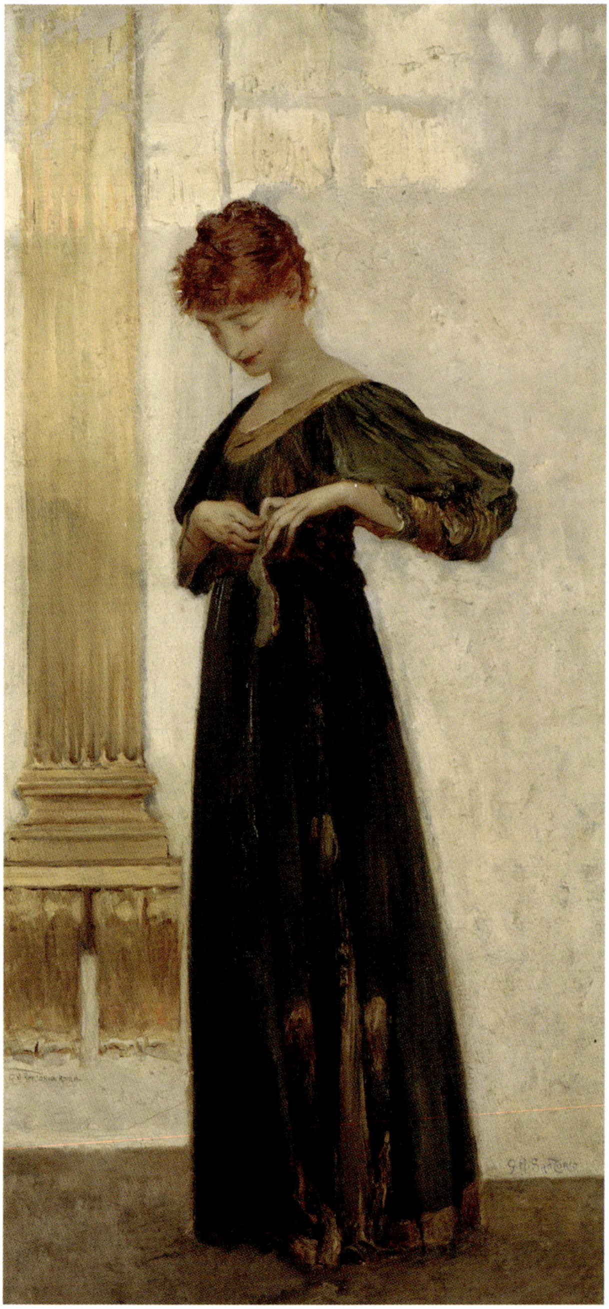

Giulio Aristide Sartorio, *Portrait of Maria Hardouin duchessa di Gallese*, 1890-1891, Rome, Galleria Nazionale d'Arte Moderna

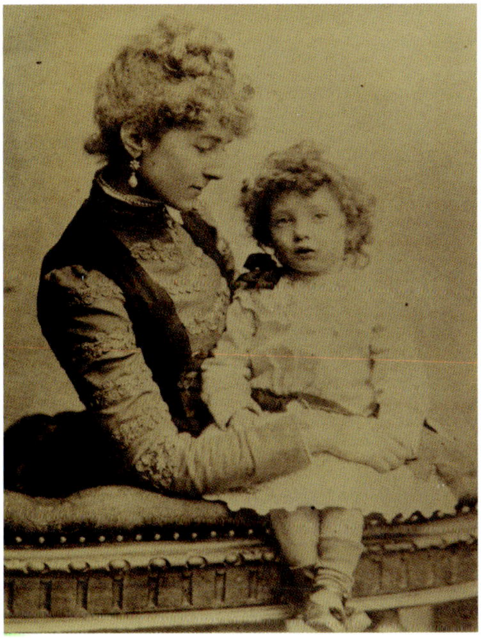

Maria Hardouin di Gallese with her firstborn child, Mario

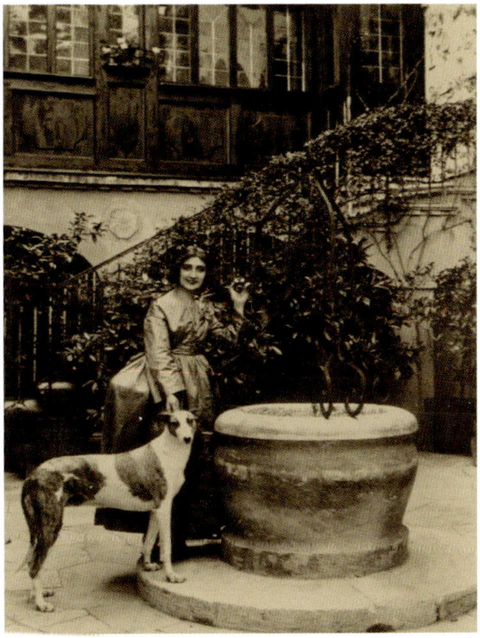

Luisa Baccara in the Cortile degli Schiavoni at the Vittoriale

holiday destination for a refined international tourist clientele since the late nineteenth century – away from Rome and Mussolini's growing power. Gabriele, who was anxious to finish the *Notturno*, declared he was "avid for silence after so much noise, and for peace after so much war," and threatened to "throw himself in the canal" if he could not find what he was looking for. The villa, which had been abandoned with all its contents in 1915, shortly before Italy's entry into the war, and had been expropriated as a result of the 1918 decree on war reparations, was the former residence of Heinrich Thode, an art historian of European fame and a student of the Italian Renaissance, who lived there with his first wife Daniela Senta von Bülow, daughter of Cosima Liszt, and later with his second wife, the violinist Herta Tegner; the grand piano in the music room had belonged to Cosima's father, Franz Liszt (it is now preserved in the museum of La Scala in Milan).

The house was relatively small (nineteen rooms) and simple, but was enchanting for the beauty of the vegetation – a grove of magnolias, olive trees, cypresses, palm trees, azaleas and roses – and the house and surrounding land immediately captivated d'Annunzio, perhaps remembering the delights of Capponcina, who signed a lease contract with the sequestrator, Giovanni Ubertazzi, Chief Tax Inspector in Brescia, for a period of a year, thereafter renewable every six months. But d'Annunzio, at fifty-eight years old, was getting tired and clearly felt that the time had come to stop and settle down, as he confessed to Antongini, "in a house where I can rest my shipwrecked remains". A few months later, on 1 October 1921, he bought the villa, farmhouse, gardener's house, orchard and olive grove for the sum of 360,000 Lire, obtained in a loan from the Bank of Rome, and repaid, from his incomes and royalties, only after his death. In 1922 and 1935 he added the oil press, the hilltop, the boating dock on the lake, and the Villa Mirabella with its outhouses to his purchase: nine hectares of land altogether, in order to guarantee sufficient space for all his needs. Villa Mirabella, for example, was home for long periods of time to the poet's wife, the duchess Maria Altemps Hardouin di Gallese: she had married d'Annunzio at

The Prioria facade during the restructuring work

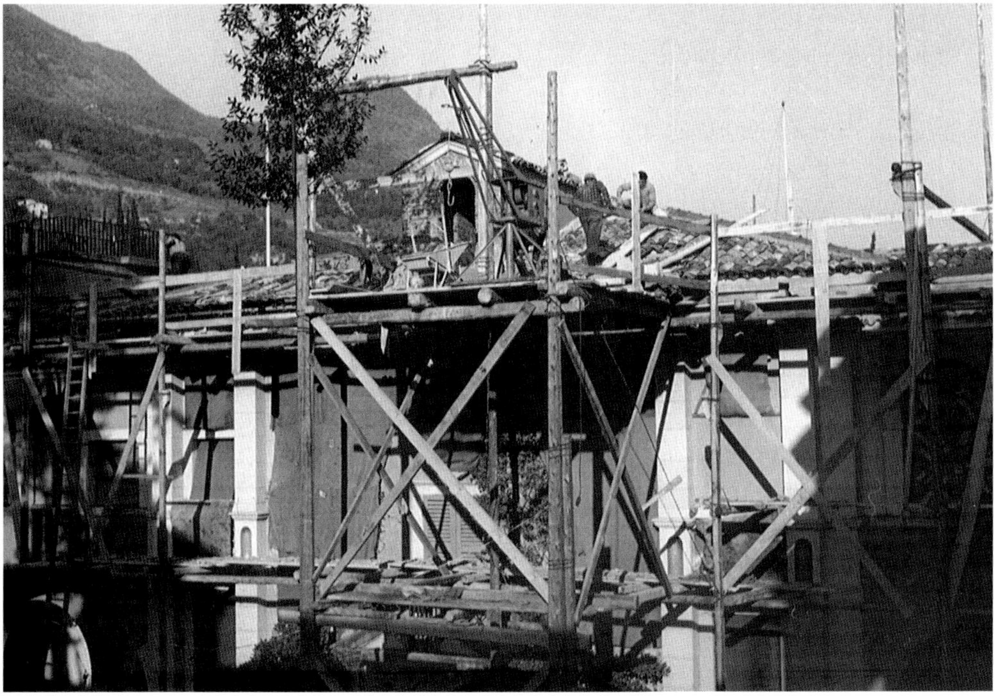

the age of nineteen and had borne him three sons, Mario, Gabriellino and Veniero; having attempted suicide as a young woman, the delicate, ethereal Maria had become resigned for some time to their *de facto* separation, but had never divorced him.
From1923, d'Annunzio christened his "estate" Il Vittoriale and ruled over it, uncontested, as prince. Indeed, he actually became a Prince, being given the title by the king in 1924, on the occasion of the annexation of Fiume. Prince of Monte Nevoso (Snowy Mountain) to be precise, after the highest mountain that marked Italy's north eastern border: the grand coat of arms with this title, displayed on the loggia that connects the *Schifamondo* to the *Torre degli Archivi*, dominates Piazza dell'Esedra.
From the moment he signed the contract, the new owner followed all the restoration work with keen interest from the Grand Hotel in Gardone not far away: the villa was very dilapidated, but d'Annunzio actually seemed quite happy about this: it meant that the game of transforming it would be all the more radical. It needed to be "de-Germanized", for, in addition to the library of over six thousand books – some of them quite rare – which was absorbed into d'Annunzio's library, Rhode had left art photographs, musical scores and some beautiful paintings, furniture and also other objects that did not suit d'Annunzio's sophisticated, anti-bourgeois taste.
The place is characterized by a rustic, exquisite simplicity and d'Annunzio was charmed by this aspect, too; since his period in Fiume, and during the years of his maturity, and of political intolerance, d'Annunzio had shown a marked "Franciscan" tendency ("I am but a mere *Poverello d'Italia* – as St Francis – and have no wish to be anything else," he wrote to Antongini on 21 October 1922, on the eve of the March on Rome). He had always been a nomad, but was also always in search of a peaceful place where he could write without being disturbed. In his youth, fleeing from love problems and the pressure of worldly affairs, he had

been given hospitality at the "Monastery", the eighteenth century building that had been de-consecrated and placed at his disposal by his friend and fellow countryman Francesco Paolo Michetti, at Francavilla al Mare; there, in happy and intense full creative flow, he had written *Il piacere* and *L'innocente*.

The poet immediately felt the same cloister-like aspect, where isolation can become maximum mental concentration, in the Cargnacco estate, which was initially called – not by chance – "Porziuncola", "Hermitage", or "Calònica". *Priory* was the name which the main residential building was finally given. On a visit to Gardone in February 1922, Ojetti mentions that during the work on the facade, two eighteenth century religious frescoes were discovered (a *Madonna with Child* and a *San Girolamo*); to extend the sacred connotations further, d'Annunzio had two notices nailed to the main doorway in "the colour of the Franciscan habit" with *Clausura* (*Seclusion*) and *Silentium* (*Silence*) written on them; "more of a desperate hope than a rule that was obeyed" comments Ojetti, knowing well that after Fiume, the poet was seeking "protection from noise, frost, sun, strangers, and politics, and the defence of his work, his books, his freedom and his memories." It was not by chance, Ojetti recalls, that among the first works he undertook as owner, "with his trench-war experience", was to surround his land with "obstacles, walls, fences and gates". The place's final aspect, after the passing of the years and through later acquisitions of surrounding land and buildings, was that of a genuine fortified citadel.

Naturally, it was a totally d'Annunzian sacredness that enveloped the place and its surroundings from this time up until the poet's death: an intellectual and secular sacredness, constructed from the cult of beauty, poetry, and art, and from the highly imaginative, grandiose personality of the writer and man of action – continually brought to the attention of the European and American public by the re-printing of his works –, and finally from a spasmodic search for love and sensuality. Indeed, d'Annunzio was followed to Gardone by the companion who was to remain with him until his death, Venetian pianist Luisa Baccara, and his French housekeeper-cum-lover Amélie Mazoyer, known as Aélis. Over the years, numerous other occasional lovers were added to these, many of them very young, attracted by the fame and generosity of the great seducer, who never tired of the pleasures of the flesh, nor of luxury.

Gian Carlo Maroni

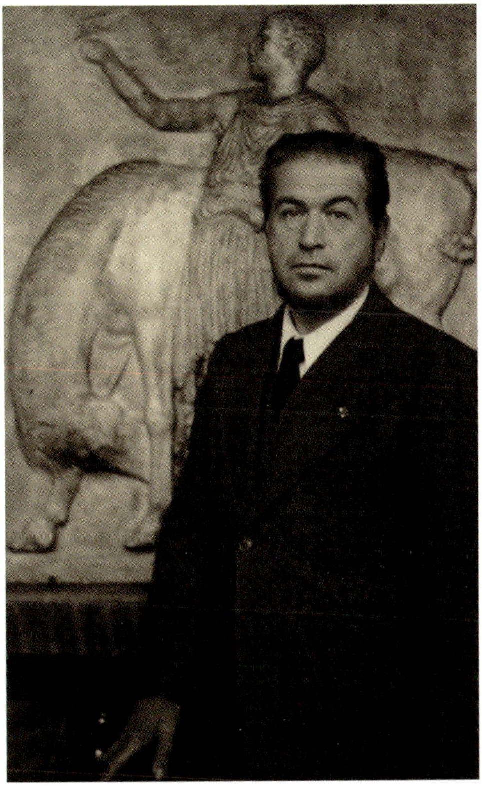

In this seductive atmosphere of beauty and culture, he did not renounce modern comforts: among the first building work that the new owner ordered was the installation of a stove heating system, a new electricity system, a telephone line; and, right from the start, furnishings and accessories of all kinds inside the new living environments.

The villa was a real building site, and d'Annunzio, with the help of the young architect Gian Carlo Maroni, the "Master of living stone" who, after d'Annunzio's death, continued the work in accordance with his directions – was a tireless creator, never completely satisfied, who moulded the environment in which he lived with the aim of making it into an immense work

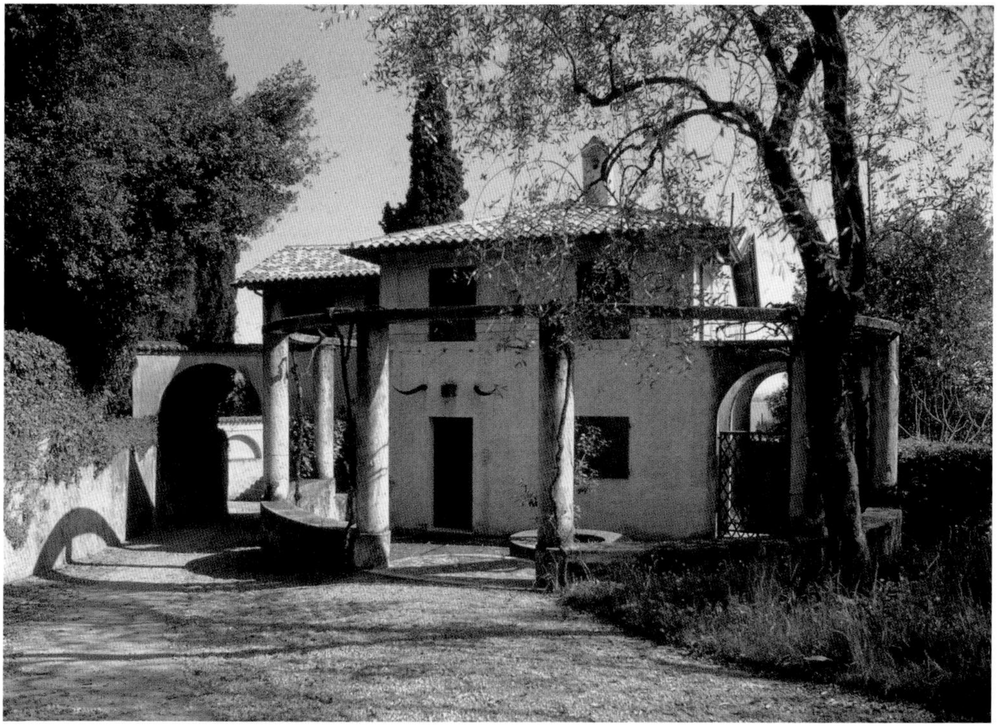

of art. "I will leave the structural framework to you, and keep the decoration for myself," Gabriele wrote to his architect. Maroni was a young man full of enthusiasm for his work and a patriot (as a volunteer he was awarded the Silver Medal during the war), and was so faithful and willing to put up with d'Annunzio's caprices, mood swings and sudden dissatisfactions that by the final years he was to become the only true "brother" to his "Commandant" (he sometimes signed himself "Brother Gian Carlo"). Numerous, often ironic letters, notes and telegrams (about two thousand documents, recently published) testify to the close relationship between the two men, which became ever more affectionate over the years, to the extent that Maroni became spokesman, accountant, *factotum* and "filter" for the shy poet (competing in this role with Luisa Baccara), and between him, as customer, and the artists and craftsmen – goldsmiths, glaziers, potters, blacksmiths, weavers and cabinet-makers – called on to participate in the "Santa Fabbrica" or "Holy Factory", as it was called, a building site that was never closed and was in perpetual ferment.

From 1934 on, Maroni lived in the *Casseretto* (*Quarterdeck*), that also housed the "Factory" offices, and from 1937 until his death in 1952, he held the post of superintendent of the Vittoriale; having fully taken on the role of custodian of d'Annunzio's wishes, he faithfully followed all his directions and even declared that he had received orders after his death, through séances. He was the obedient executor of his client's orders, but was also respectful of the architectural style of the area – in the use of square columns and loggias with rounded arches, for example – and was attentive to the Art Déco, rationalist, twentieth century trends that dominated the architecture of the time. Marcello Piacentini, the great architect and neo-classical urban developer, devoted an article to *Gian Carlo Maroni, architect of the Vittoriale* in the December 1930 issue of the magazine

Gardone Sopra,
the buildings opposite
the Vittoriale, later
knocked down to create
the Piazza dei Caduti

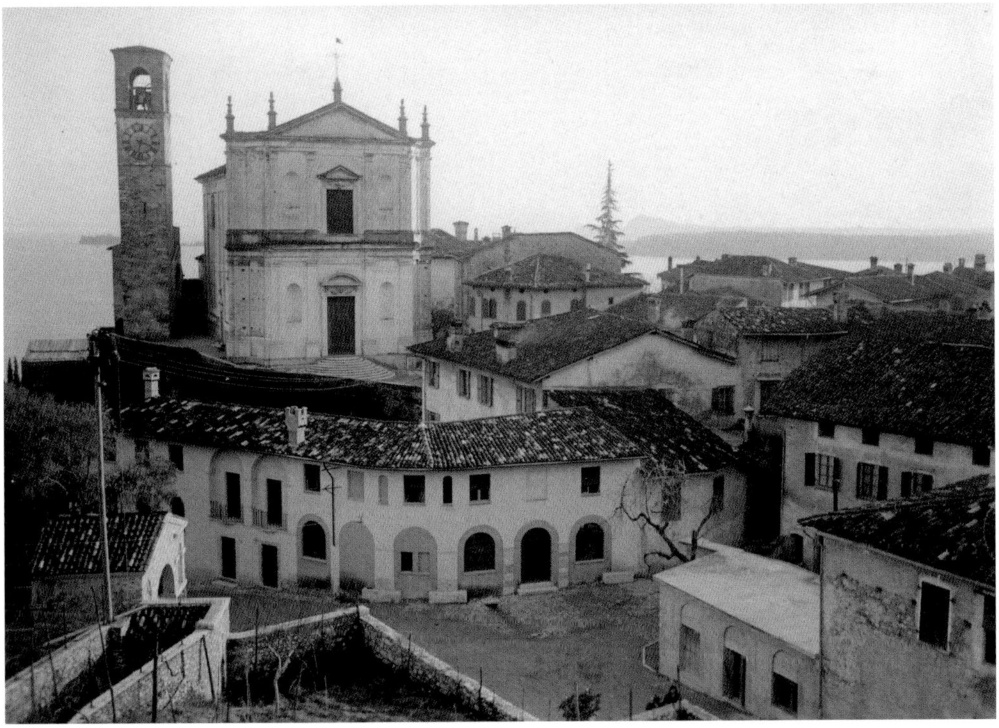

"Architecture and the decorative Arts", which he edited together with Gustavo Giovannoni; and it was Piacentini who had left free copies of the first three years' issues of the magazine when he visited the Vittoriale in August 1925, so d'Annunzio knew the magazine well.
For his part, d'Annunzio was equally hard at work, devoting himself to the "decorations", guiding purchases and commissioning artefacts, and from self-taught amateur he ventured into various forms of craftsmanship: "I beat out iron, blow glass, engrave semi-precious stones, print wood with a press, colour fabrics, carve bone and box-wood, make subtle perfumes," we read in the deed of gift of the villa. But above all, he carefully considered decorations, combinations, and creations like a genuine artist, devoting the same tireless and obsessive care with which, as a young man, he had consulted dictionaries and bibliographies to find an unusual word, or the precise, irreplaceable adjective to ornament his prose and poetry: "The supreme art inspires me, the taste for form and colour leads me in the choice and composition, an ingenious shrewdness enlightens me over how to regulate spaces and heights [...] the simple people around me smile in ignorance or astonishment, as I impatiently ask for an old nail, a piece of precious fabric, a remnant of gold ribbon, a box of water colours [...]" he wrote in 1935, in the fascinating *Cento e cento e cento e cento pagine del libro segreto di Gabriele d'Annunzio tentato di morire* (*Hundreds and hundreds and hundreds and hundreds of pages of the secret book of Gabriele D'Annunzio tempted to die*). Again, as proof of a real "physical" and carnal love for a work of art, for a sublime artefact chosen from among many, in one of the thousands of notes preserved in the Vittoriale archives we read: "I like to free the objects of art that I like best from the dust, to warm them up – to revive them – with my breath and my touch."
The product of so much passion, so many creative touches and years of work, must inevitably be a mag-

Leopoldo
Metlicovitz,
Cabiria, 1914

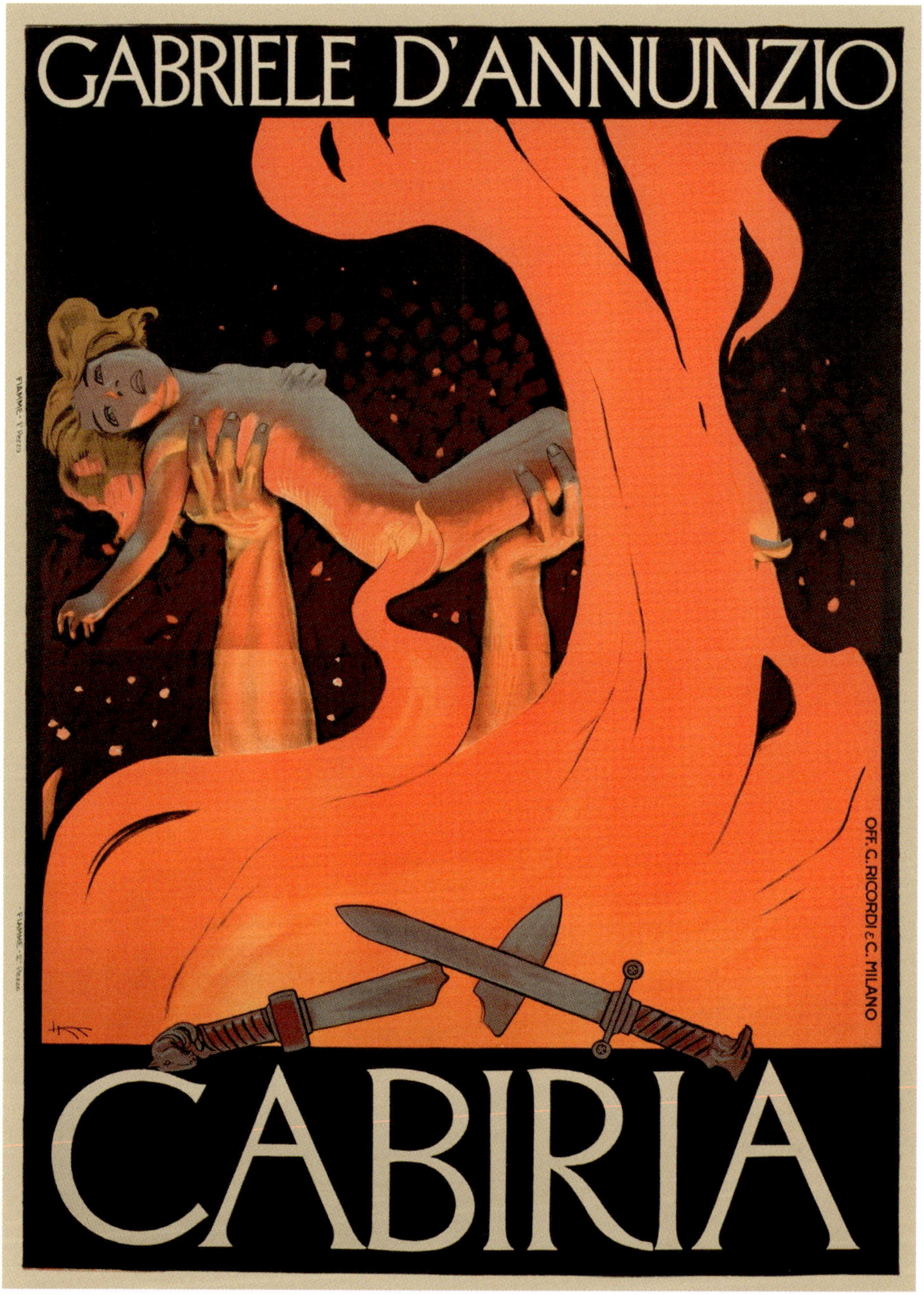

nificent and heterogeneous whole, in which the ancient and modern, the true and false, the West and the East dialogue together in a continual interplay of cultural and figurative references, citations, and recollections; so it is not surprising to find in the rooms of the Vittoriale copies and casts of the Parthenon horses, of Phidias's *Athena Lemnia*, of Praxiteles's *Hermes*, of *Samothrace's Nike*, or of Michelangelo's *Dying Prisoner*; nor is it astonishing to see the numerous architectural and decorative allusions: the arches of the avenues leading to the villa reminiscent of Roman aqueducts, or the *Parlaggio* which imitates the amphitheatre in Pompei. D'Annunzio was perfectly capable of discernment, and showed a highly sensitive and curious taste for contemporary artists, for example; it was certainly not deceit or self-deception on his part, but the desire to mix past and present, fiction and truth poetically, in a perpetual, surprising stage set.

The huge economic expenditure that was necessary for all this, and for the thousands of comforts and personal vices which d'Annunzio indulged in – the perfumes and clothes (hundreds of silk shirts, fur coats, shoes, and dressing gowns), the women and the frequent use of "silly powder" (as he called cocaine) – was made possible by the earnings from the publication and reprinting of his works. *Notturno* was published in 1921, achieving extraordinarily successful sales, and in 1927 Mondadori publishes the national edition of d'Annunzio's works, making a total of 48 volumes altogether. But the money also came from articles published in the Italian and American press which were generously paid, from the royalties received from works for the theatre and cinema (he received the remarkable sum of 50,000 Lire, as payment for inventing the names of the characters and the captions for *Cabiria*, the first great film of Italian cinema made in 1914), or from sales of his autograph. But the government aid made directly available by Mussolini also played a large part. Mussolini, who was directly inspired by d'Annunzio's forcefulness and by many of his ideas, had opposed feelings of admiration and diffidence for him, and observed him through his emissary, police chief Antonio Rizzo: the latter acted as a "go-between" between him and the government, initially requested by d'Annunzio himself, who, during his sullen retirement from politics, had continual economic requests to present.

To cement the difficult and controversial relationship, together with the dependence on the Italian State, in December 1923 d'Annunzio gave the Vittoriale to Italy: not yet complete and not yet paid for, but still, in the mind of the poet, the last and most complete of his artistic creations. "I have donated the Vittoriale, full of holy relics and precious objects. I am the sad custodian," he wrote in 1932.

Custodian, craftsman, creator; we read in the notary Act of donation: "Not only every house I have furnished and every room I have carefully arranged, but every object that I have chosen and collected in different periods of my life was always a means of expression, a means of spiritual revelation for me, like one of my poems or one of my plays, like any political or military act, like any of my testimonies to upright, indomitable faith. That is why I dare to offer the Italian people all that remains to me, and all that I may buy from now onwards to improve my restoration work. [...] Everything here has been created and transfigured by me. Everything here shows the imprint of my style in the sense that I want to give to my style [...]. Everything here is a form of my mind, an aspect of my spirit, a proof of my fervour."

A year after the donation the Vittoriale was declared a national monument and the Foundation was established a year before his death on 1 March 1938. Even while d'Annunzio was still alive, the place had become the focus of attention for visits by friends, politicians, intellectuals and the curious, and the focus of photographic *reportages* – in other words, the focus of a genuine cultural tourism.

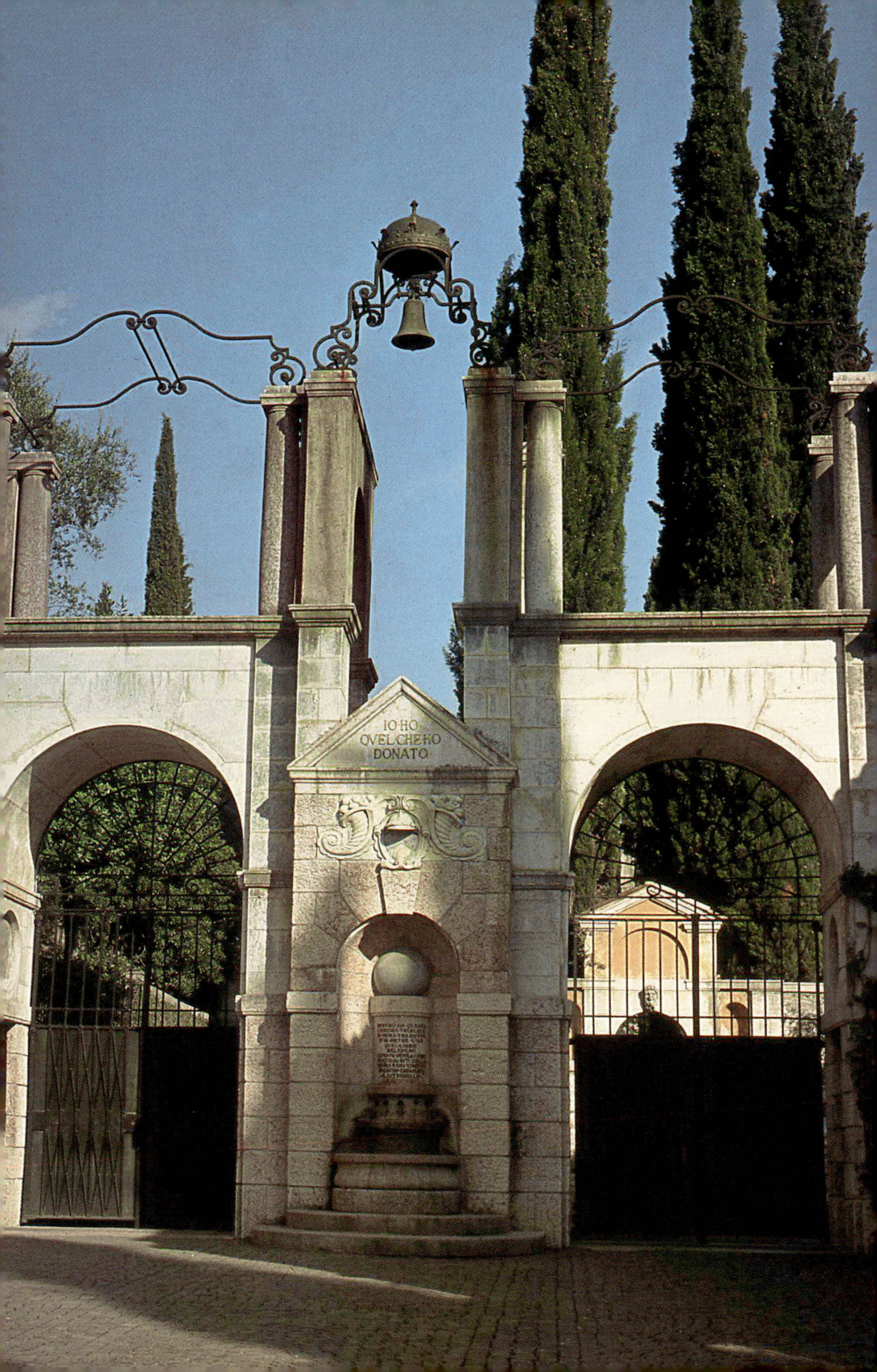
IO HO
QVEL CHE HO
DONATO

Itinerary

"After too many imperfect years I have reconstructed the interior of my universe; and I am the only lord of it. [...] I create, transfigure, invent [...]."

Gabriele d'Annunzio, *Le cento e cento e cento e cento pagine del libro segreto di Gabriele d'Annunzio tentato di morire*

The Piazza, the Entrance and the War Memorial

Built by Gian Carlo Maroni in 1931 to connect the property to the surrounding area, the arcades and loggia of the First World War Memorial draws on the typical architectural styles of the area.

D'Annunzio, who was longing for peace and solitude, was disturbed by the church bells ("the obscenity of the bells" he called it, in 1924 offering the parish priest 8000 Lire a year to stop ringing them), but most of all by the din, the low-life clientele and "wine-soaked racket" of a nearby "vile restaurant", and in 1933 he obtained permission from the Government to have it knocked down, thus securing the whole area around the Vittoriale. So, as the years passed, it became a closed fortress, accessed by a double doorway: one road, which is steep and narrow (thus symbolizing the inherent difficulty of reaching the heart of knowledge), leads to the Prioria, to the new wing of the Schifamondo (with the Auditorium and the War Museum), and to the Archive buildings. The other road, which is broad and downward sloping, leads to the less "conceptual" and difficult area: the Theatre, the Casseretto, and the Villa Mirabella for guests.

"Io ho quel che ho donato" ("I have what I have given") is written on the tympanum above the central fountain at the entrance. It is a translation of a Latin hemistich by the Roman poet Rabirius, quoted by Seneca in *De beneficiis* ("hoc habeo quodcumque dedi"); quoted in a seventeenth century treatise as the motto of a sixteenth century Spanish knight, d'Annunzio saw it engraved on the hearthstone of a fifteenth century fireplace. It was one of d'Annunzio's favourite mottos and was used by him from 1916 onwards, imprinted in seals, on letter heads and in all d'Annunzio's works published by the National Institute. Written inside a circle dominated in the centre by a cornucopia, the symbol of abundance. The motto alludes to the principles of generosity and munificence which characterized the years he spent at Gardone, but in the play on words between "avere" (have) and "donare" (give), Gabriele is also alluding to the exchange agreement which he made with the government and directly with Mussolini: subsidies and money to build and furnish the place where the poet lived, but which at the same time he was donating to the State. Below this, between two cornucopias, is the coat of arms of the Prince of Monte Nevoso, the title which King Vittorio Emanuele III conferred on d'Annunzio in 1924, in recognition of his irredentist undertakings. Designed by Guido Marussig, it shows a foot soldier's helmet encircled by a laurel wreath, the seven stars of the Great Bear in a blue field and the outline of the Monte Nevoso mountain. This mountain, the highest peak in the upper Karst, which was given to d'Annunzio and is now in Slovenia near the border with Croatia, at that time marked the border of the recent annexation of Fiume. The niche below contains the fountain, with a quotation from d'Annunzio's *Libro segreto* in bronze lettering: "Inside this triple circle of walls, is the translation into living stone of the religious book that I believe directs the rites of the fatherland, called by the Latin conquerors the Vittoriale." Thus, this "book" written in "living stone", the Vittoriale, is presented to the visitor as a work of art, the last, magnificent proof of a great writer and great man, in which precious objects, relics of war and heroism, architecture, mottos, allusions and personal quotations, create a "sacred" depiction, dense with symbols and memories.

Piazzetta of the Victory of the Piave

Beyond the gateway, going in the direction of the Prioria, you come to the small piazza dedicated to the victory of the Piave which, a year after the Caporetto tragedy, confirmed Italy's final victory over the Austro-Hungarians. Standing on the *Pilum of the Piave,* which is made of stone from Torre del Benaco, is the great bronze statue of Victory, with bound feet, by sculptor Arrigo Minerbi (it is a copy of the 1917 original), donated in 1935 by the Milan city council. The statue is a female nude, arms clasped across her chest and wings raised, who is prevented from flight by the chains binding her ankles. The allusion here is to the difficult defence of the river in that fateful October of 1918, when the waters were swollen making conditions very dangerous for the swimmers from the élite army storm troops the

Entrance
of the Vittoriale

The "Dare in brocca"
Pilum and the "Piave"
Pilum with Minerbi's
Victory statue

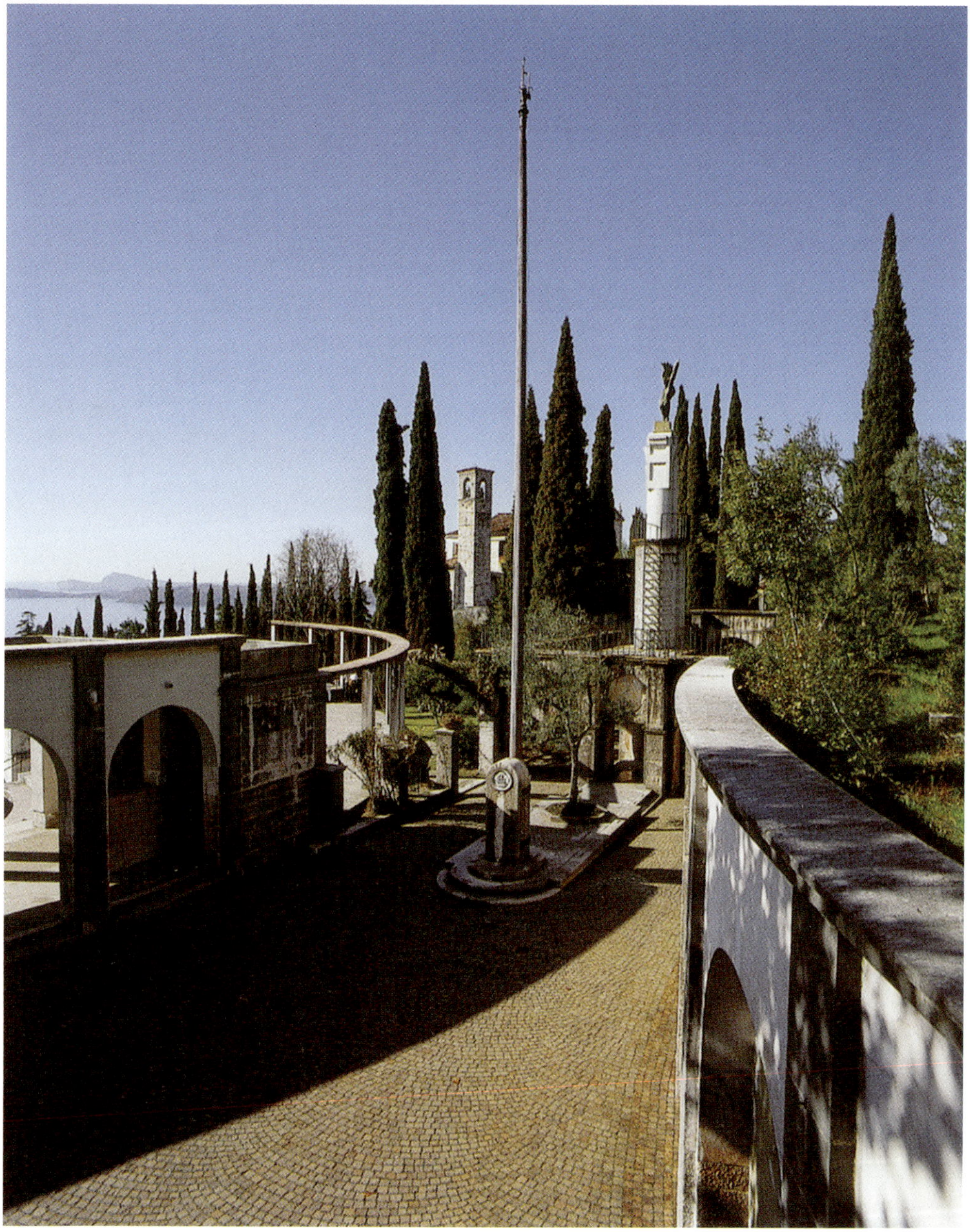

"Dare in brocca"
Pilum with the coat
of arms designed
by Guido Marussig

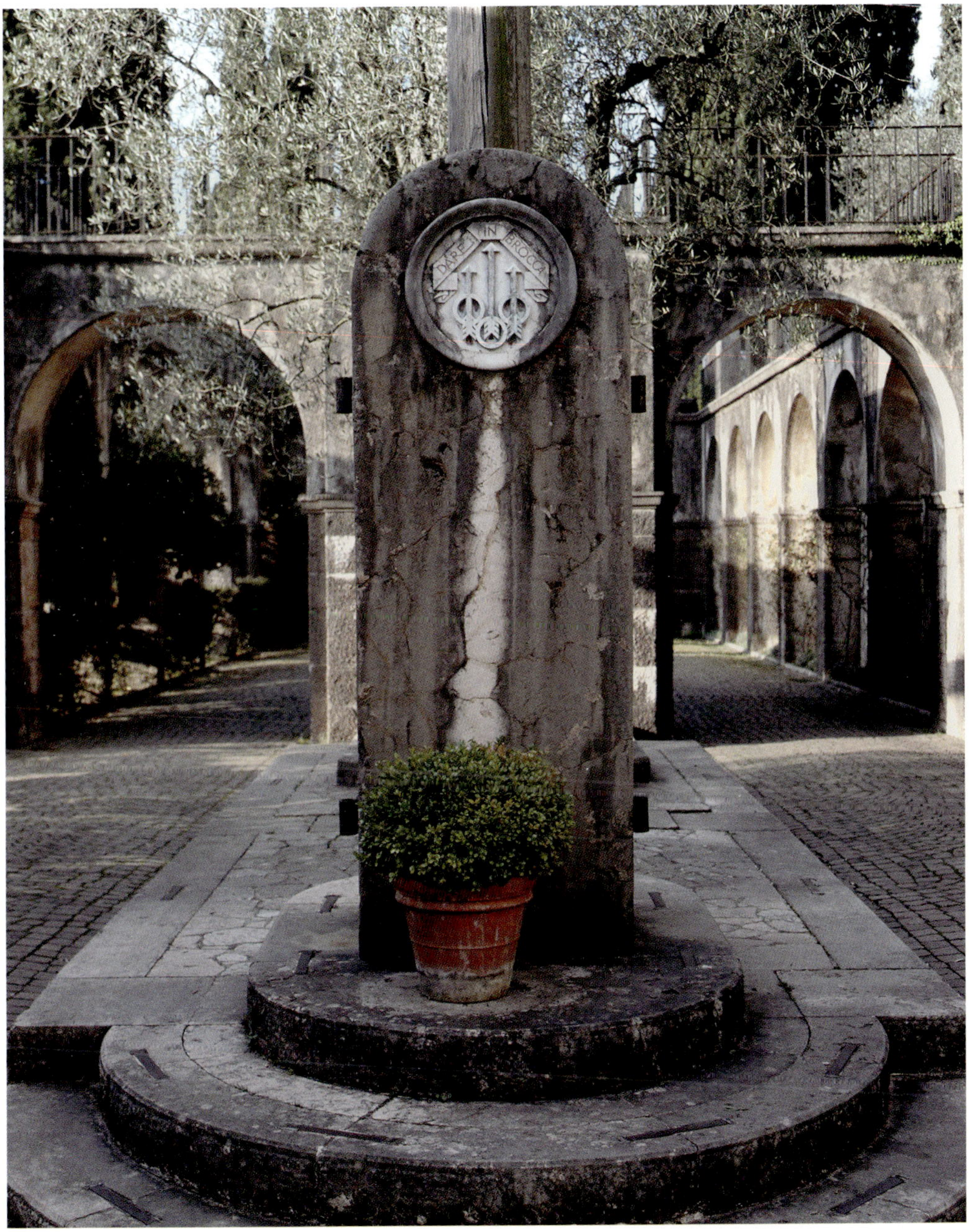

Arrigo Minerbi,
Victory of the Piave

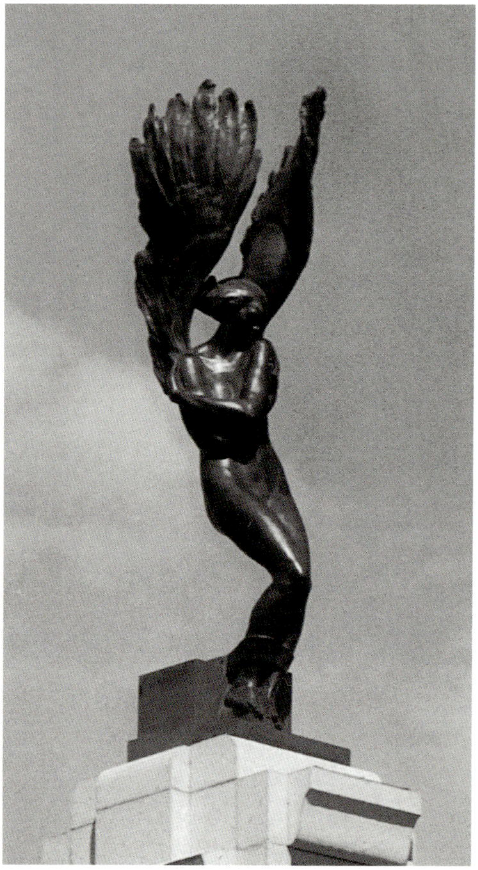

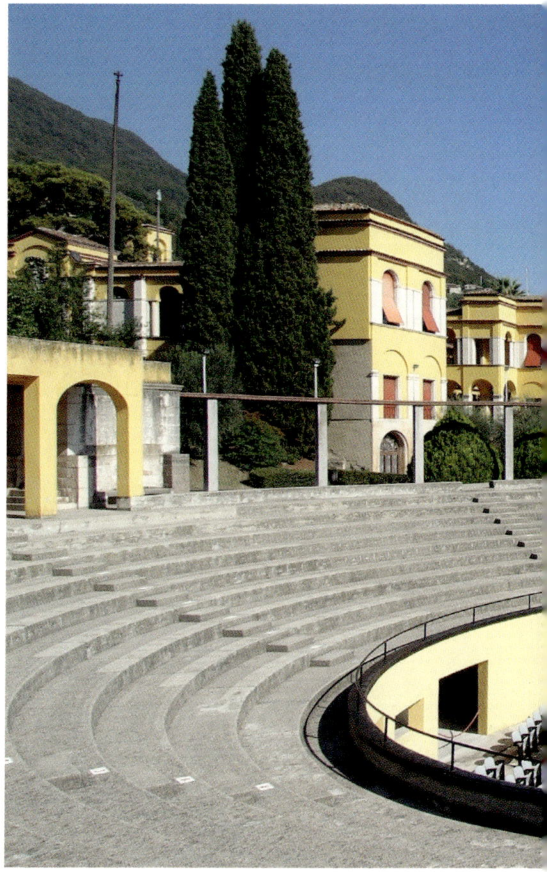

"Arditi", (known as "the Piave caimans"), who nevertheless managed to maintain the communications. There is another symbol of deliverance, alluding to the Italian victories of the First World War and the conquest of Fiume, immediately behind, in the *Pilum del "dare in brocca"*, used to hoist flags and banners. In nautical terminology "dare in brocca" means to hit the target, and this is the idea alluded to in the marble medallion with three arrows, designed by Guido Marussig.

Parlaggio

"The avenue to the right leads towards the open air theatre now under construction, with the arena supported by four deep arches and the stage framed against the background of olive trees and the lake [...]"; that is how Ugo Ojetti describes it in one of his memoirs, dated 26 August 1936. Ever since the end of the nineteenth century, debates and experiments were taking place all over Europe with the aim of bringing classical theatre back to the ancient Greek and Roman theatres. In Italy, these tendencies were supported by men of culture such as the poet Angiolo Orvieto, founder of the Florence magazine "Il Marzocco". In fact it was in this magazine that d'Annunzio expanded on Orvieto's convictions, on several occasions advocating the use, founding or restoration of open-air theatres as the ideal place for performances of ancient plays; during the period of his love affair and intellectual partnership with Eleonora Duse,

Parlaggio

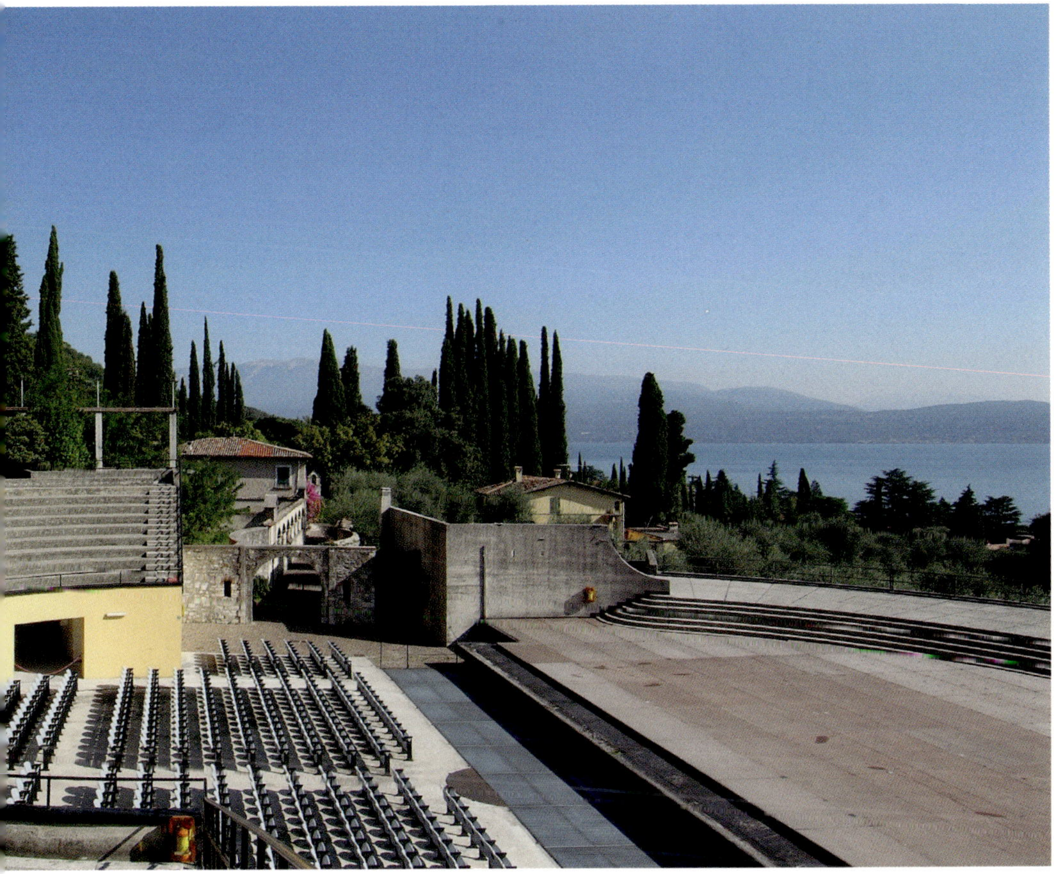

d'Annunzio had cherished the idea of building an open-air theatre on the hills around Lake Albano, near Rome, but it was only at the Vittoriale that he succeeded in realising his long-held dream. In order to be able to stage his works adequately, having occasionally staged them in the Gardens, d'Annunzio was, by 1927, already planning to build a large amphitheatre, inspired by the Greek theatre in Taormina and the Roman theatre in Pompei. In 1931, Maroni and the sculptor Renato Brozzi left for Pompei, to study the theatre and get inspiration. The result was the *Parlaggio*, "the flame beneath the whole Vittoriale complex" as the architect Piacentini wrote; with a seating capacity of 1500 spectators, it was started in 1934 and only completed in 1952; the internal corridors, for example, were to be painted with stories connected with the world of the theatre, both ancient and modern. With a splendid view over the lake, with the island of Garda and the promontory of Sirmione at the centre and the Rocca di Manerba to the right, it is still active, with a theatre summer season.

Esedra

After skirting a green area with cypresses, magnolias, and cherry laurels, and passing a Karst boulder that stands as a perpetual reminder of the harsh territory where d'Annunzio fought during the First World War, you arrive in a semi-circular piazza bounded by arches,

Tazio Nuvolari
at the Vittoriale,
April 1932

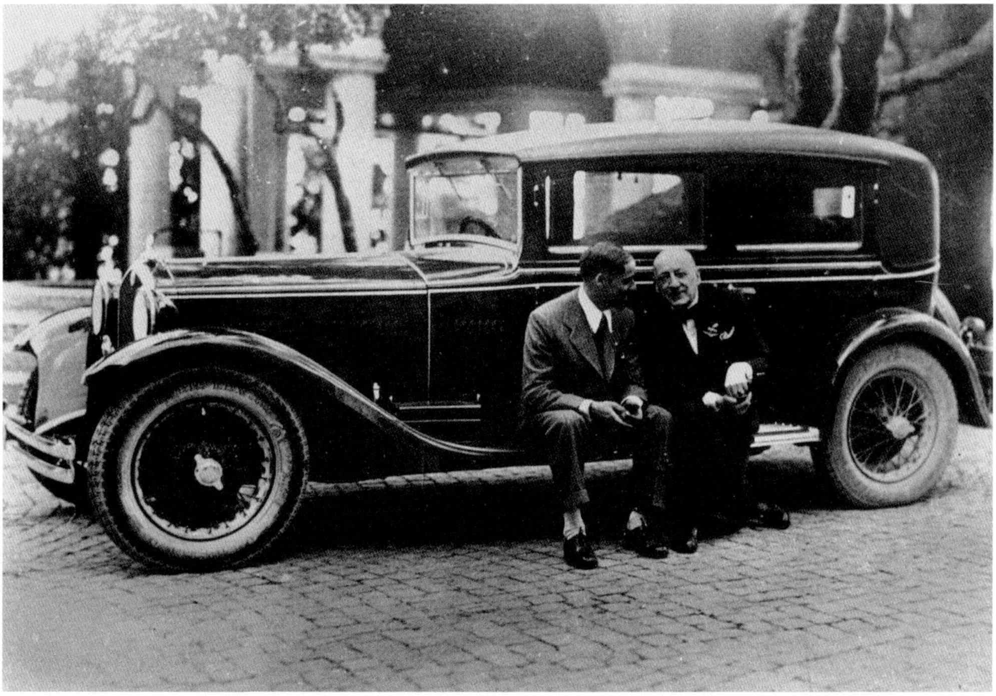

with, at the centre, the coat of arms and the motto taken from Horace: "Immotus nec iners" ("still but not inert"), alluding to d'Annunzio's situation – in voluntary reclusion, yet still alert. This is the site of the "Tempietto delle memorie dannunziane" (Temple of d'Annunzian Memories), constructed in 1934, with bas-reliefs on the outside walls by Napoleone Martinuzzi, the sculptor and Venetian glasswork master, depicting views of the towns of Zadar and Split, a copy of the sixteenth century bas relief on the outside of the church of Santa Maria del Giglio in Venice. To complete the record of important places in d'Annunzio's life are some stone slabs, donated at various times by the city authorities of Pola, Fiume and Pescara. D'Annunzio's remains, now in the Mausoleum, were preserved inside the Tempietto until 1963, and there are still numerous mementos in there, for example, the bronze crown from the Italian Royal Academy, of which the poet was appointed president in 1937, and the Roman amphora containing water from the river Piave. Under the portico are two of d'Annunzio's cars, which the poet loved to drive at great speed along the roads around the lake: the black and red *Fiat type 4*, with which he set off to conquer Fiume between 11 and 12 September (with a crest designed by Guido Marussig showing the transfer of the Holy house of Loreto), and a wonderfully elegant, blue *Torpedo Isotta Fraschini*. The piazza is surrounded by a simple covered passageway linking the Palazzo di Schifamondo with the Torre degli Archivi.

Piazzetta Dalmata

This small piazza is dominated by a pilum on top of which stands the *Virgin with the Sceptre of Dalmatia* (the original, in copper embossed on wood, was replaced in 1964 by this bronze copy). On the plinth, made from two millstones from an old olive press, are eight late-sixteenth century bearded heads, set into it like a crown. A long inscription commemorates the nine years since Italy's entry into the First World War on 24 May 1915, and seven years since the battle be-

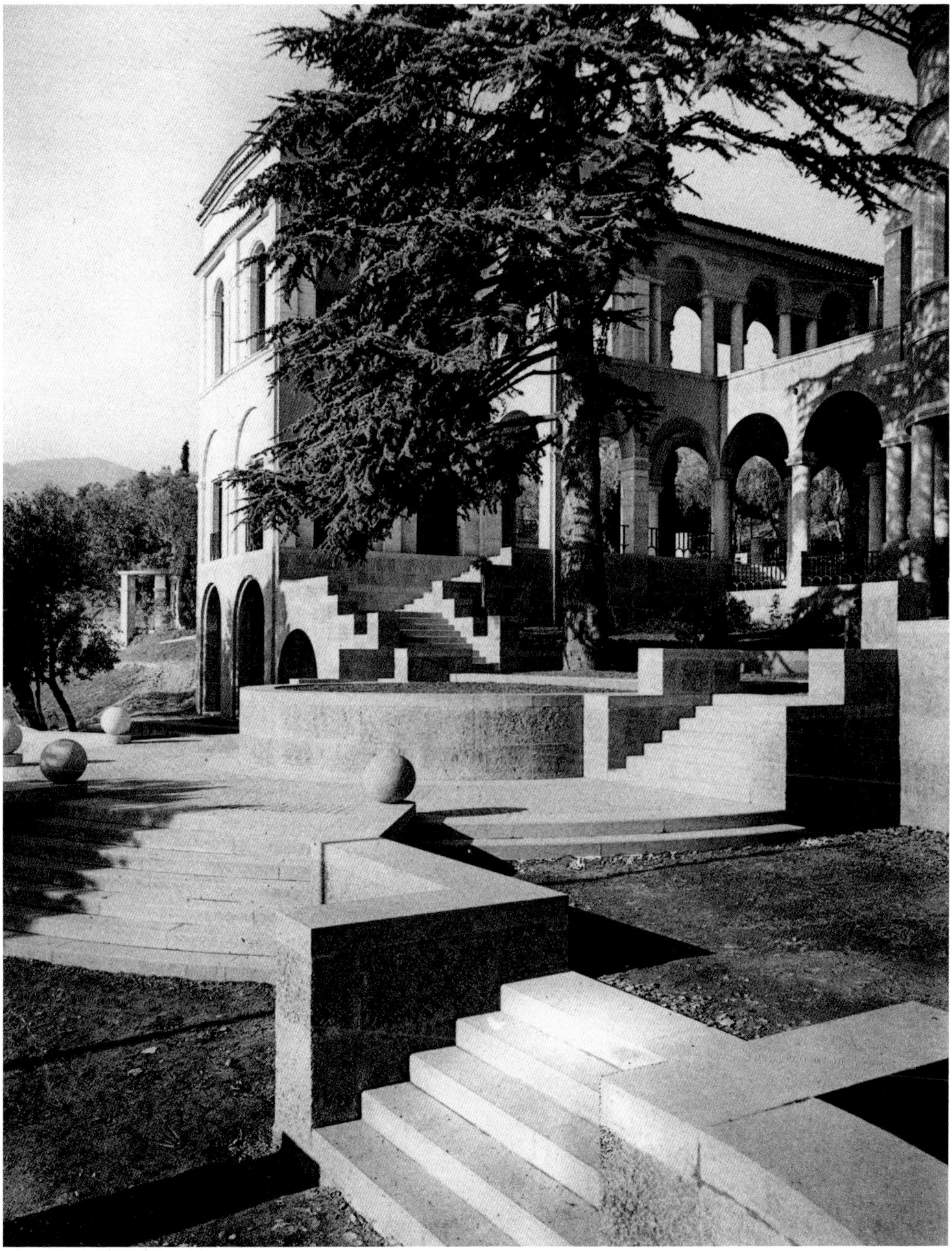

The Torre degli Archivi and the loggias leading to Schifamondo

Sketch of the greyhound
coat of arms
designed by d'Annunzio

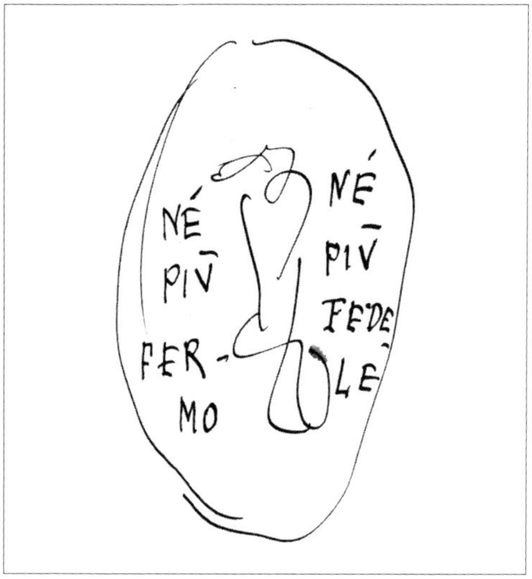

tween the Austro-Hungarian and Italian troops on 27 May 1917 at the source of the Timavo; it was during this battle that Major Giovanni Randaccio, commander of the "Tuscan Wolves" battalion, died heroically in d'Annunzio's arms.

The inscription reads: "Praise and glory be / To the Blessed Virgin of the Sceptre of Dalmatia / Who for the eight winds of the Italian rose / As for these eight skulls / Re-conquered the barbarian slave. / From the first rampart of Rome on the Adrante mountain / To the bloody altars of Mark / In the labyrinth of Cattaro/ And from that rough overhanging rock / As far as the summit of the Acroceraunii/ Do not learn from the love of destiny and lightning / Ninth anniversary of the declaration of war / Seventh of the Pentecost on the Timavo / XXIV May MCMXV-MCMXXIV/ XXVII May MCMXVII-MCMXXIV/ and beyond."

Two buildings face onto the piazza: in the centre is the Prioria, the older building, restored and enlarged, where Gabriele lived. On the left is Schifamondo, the new wing that was completed by the architect, Maroni, only after the poet's death, and whose name, inspired by the Palazzo Schifanoia in Ferrara (which was also the name he gave to a magnificent building described in *Il Piacere*), alludes to his reclusive life in Gardone and to the feeling of being "tired of the world" that characterized the poet's last years. On the right is the Archivi building, and a fountain designed by Maroni. The entrance to the Gardens is beside the arcade with stone seats known as *dell'obolo (of the obol)*, and in the arcades it is the Belvedere niche in which there is a copy of the Greek bronze statue of *Winged Victory* (without the wings) preserved in the Brescia Museum of Art and History (1st century B.C.), which was donated in 1934 by the Brescia ex-Servicemen. Also on the right is a stairway leading down to the lake; the tomb of Gabriele's wife, the Duchess Maria Hardouin di Gallese (1864-1954), is nearby.

Casseretto

The Casseretto was the site of the "Holy Factory" offices; this small villa with a semi-circular colonnaded pronaos, designed and built by Gian Carlo Maroni – it was later to become his home – now houses the Vittoriale Headquarters, and is excluded from the tour itinerary. In nautical terminology, the "casseretto", or quarterdeck, is the covered area at the stern of a ship where the living quarters are.

Villa Mirabella

Among the purchases made in 1924 was the Villa Mirabella, the former San Damiano, which is also excluded from the tour itinerary. After having changed the furnishings, d'Annunzio used this villa to accommodate the artists involved in the decoration work on the Vittoriale, the librarian, Antonio Brunes, and his own wife, Maria, who moved to the Prioria after the death of her husband.

Prioria

The "Prioria" was the old Villa Cargnacco and was d'Annunzio's true sanctuary, a sacred place that was spiritual in a secular way, a symbolic monument to the living poet. The façade is studded with coats of arms (Canossa, Medici, and the cities of Trieste, Trento, and Turin), and, in accordance with the poet's wishes, is reminiscent of the Palazzo del Podestà in Arezzo and like many Venetian municipal buildings: "It should be studded with stones without any symmetrical arrangement," Gabriele stipulated in 1925.

At the centre is a coat of arms with a greyhound – symbolizing faithfulness and independence – and the

Prioria's facade

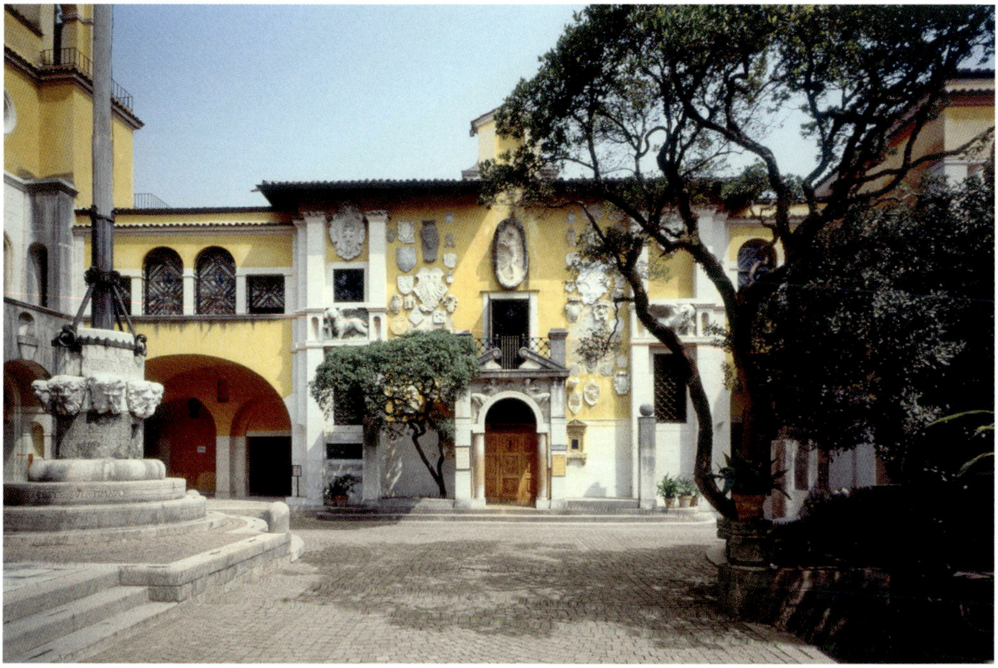

motto "none more steadfast, none more faithful", designed by d'Annunzio himself. On the entrance archway are two representations of *Victory* or allegories of *Fame* by the Sansovino school, resting on the arch, with an inscription expressing this wish: "May there be peace in this home. Spirit of Victory give peace to the house of a valiant man." Then, inscribed on the wooden architrave, are the words: "Seclusion until he opens – Silence until he speaks". On the ground floor are high reliefs of the *Lion of Saint Mark*, the *Eagle of St John,* and a high relief in bronze with the lines from the *Canticle of the Creatures* by St. Francis of Assisi: "Praise be to you, my lord, for our sister Mother Earth....", to which d'Annunzio added the final verse: "And blessed are those who die in a good war". Monastic peace and silence, therefore, chosen with the scorn and rejection that the poet felt for the world, but also a reminder of, and allusion to, victory; but it is a truncated victory, mutilated like the *Winged Victory* (with no arms) attached to the doorway, made by Trieste-born Guido Marussig.

Vestibule

This is the entrance to the house, accessed by passing through a gilded wrought-iron gate and walking up seven steps (the number of the Virtues and Vices), the "mystical stairway" as Gabriele called it in his letters to Maroni. Before going up, on the right, is a niche with the *Annunciation*, an enamelled copper by Giuseppe Guidi recalling the poet's name – Gabriele d'Annunzio: the archangel Gabriel who "announced" the birth of Christ. On the landing is a stone column with the symbols of the passion at its base, and above it a golden basket full of pomegranates. This fruit, an ancient symbol of abundance and prosperity but also evoking the blood and passion of Christ, can be found in several places in the house, made from different materials. Halfway up the stairs are two gold plaster lions, a crosier, a holy water font, and a wooden *Triptych of the Virgin, Saint Francis and Saint Anthony*. Above are three pairs of wooden angels holding lamps in the form of cornucopias, and two plaster heads. At the bottom is a greeting with the words "te hospitio agresti accipiemus"

Vestibule

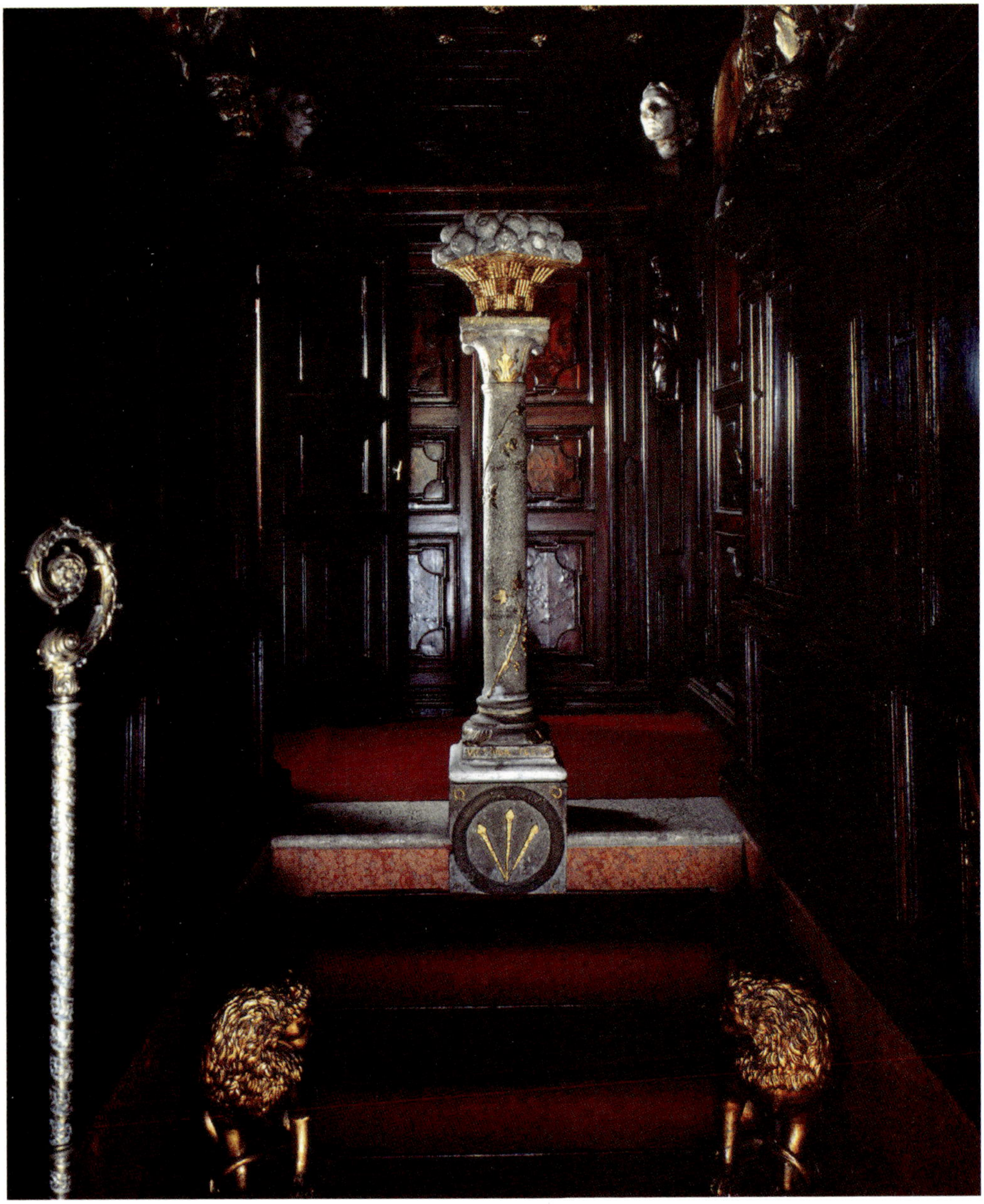

Music Room

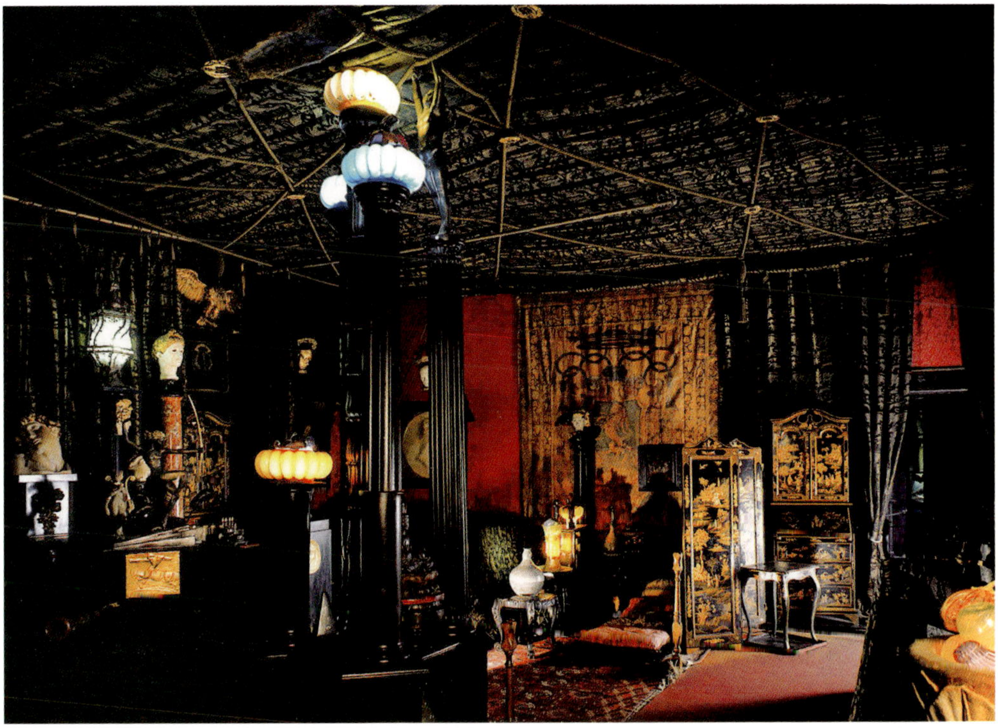

("We welcome you to this country retreat") (taken from Cicero's *Letter to Atticus*). Two doors lead onto to other passage areas: on the left is the Dalmatian Oratory, with ("nihil coinquinatum", "nothing is contaminated" inscribed on the door), and on the right the *Stanza del Mascheraio (Masking Room)*. The lunettes on the door depict *Saint Francis* and *Saint Claire*, and were painted by the Salò artist Angelo Landi, in 1925.

Stanza del Mascheraio (Masking Room)

In the 1930s, this room was used as a waiting room for less welcome guests. The mirror is inscribed with these words: "To the visitor. Do you bring with you the mirror of Narcissus? / This is leaded glass or a masking mirror. / Adjust your mask on your face / but consider that you are glass against steel." This severe warning seems to have been directed particularly at Mussolini. On the walls, on shelves designed by Maroni, are books and musical scores that belonged to Heinrich Thode and ceramics by the Faenza artist Pietro Melandri, one of the greatest ceramics artists of the twentieth century. A gramophone, a radio and some records bear witness to the poet's interest in light music, jazz, fox trots, spirituals, rumba, and the songs of the famous singer Josephine Baker. The bronze horse by French designer Edmond Etling, on the table and a Murano glass chandelier in the shape of a cornucopia, by Napoleone Martinuzzi, testify to d'Annunzio's taste for the most elegant decorative trends of his time.

Stanza della Musica (Music Room)

Also called the "Gasparo Room" (named after the luthier of Salò who considered himself the inventor of the violin), the room was started in 1926 and completed in 1929, and was designed to host concerts by Luisa Baccara and the strings of the "Vittoriale Quartet" called sometimes from Venice; it is one of the most complex and richly decorated rooms in the Prioria, fascinating in

Adolfo De Carolis,
Dantes Adriaticus,
1920

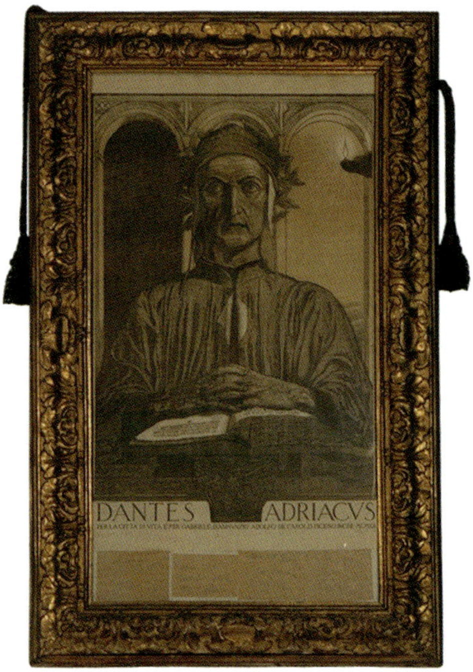

its intermingling of references and the many different works of art it contains. It is divided up, like a musical phrase, by fifteen columns; a bronze Eros stands on one of the tallest, a copy of the statue in the Bargello museum in Florence by Iacopo Alari Bonacolsi known as the Elder, which seems to support the fabric of the ceiling. On the other columns are sculptures of various different origins and materials, including the splendid orange and blue *Luminous pumpkins*, and the *Baskets of fruit*, by the Murano glass master Napoleone Martinuzzi; they are unusual objects which, with their opalescent pieces of coloured glass, shed a beautiful light over the whole room. The light is all the more unusual when the alabaster window screens by Pietro Chiesa – a Milanese stained glass expert and founder of the famous Fontana Arte lighting company, together with Gio Ponti in 1933 – are completely lowered.

The ceiling is entirely covered with black silk drapes embroidered with silver, made by Vittorio Ferrari for the Florence manufacturers Giuseppe Lisio – a company specializing in velvet, brocade and reproductions of antique fabrics; they are inspired by oriental and medieval fabrics depicting wild animals – rhinoceroses, gazelles and fawns – (in fact, the fabric is called "belluato" or wild). The walls are covered with a pink damask fabric; beneath are some high-backed monastic stalls made of walnut wood with scrolls inscribed with the words "Vigilia et labor" and "Pax et quies". There are various paintings hanging on the walls, some antique (a portrait by the Florentine Mannerist painter Agnolo Bronzino, another attributed to Giovan Girolamo Savoldo, another by an artist of the Raphaelesque school, and a sixteenth century *Madonna with Child* by a German school), and some modern (the *Portrait of Cosima Liszt* in charcoal and white lead, by the famous Munich artist Franz von Lenbach), and a fine leather tapestry with the Altemps coat of arms that came from the Rome residence of d'Annunzio's wife, Maria Hardouin.

One object with direct links to d'Annunzio's life story is the *Dantes Adriaticus*, a large woodcut by Adolfo De Carolis, one of d'Annunzio's favourite contemporary artists and the illustrator of many of his works, which was created in 1920 on the occasion of the conquest of Fiume (the original wood block is in the *Officina*).

D'Annunzio, who came from Pescara, referred to himself as the "Dante of the Adriatic", in fact, claiming somewhat immodestly in one of his notes: "Italian po-

Napoleone
Martinuzzi,
Luminous
pumpkins

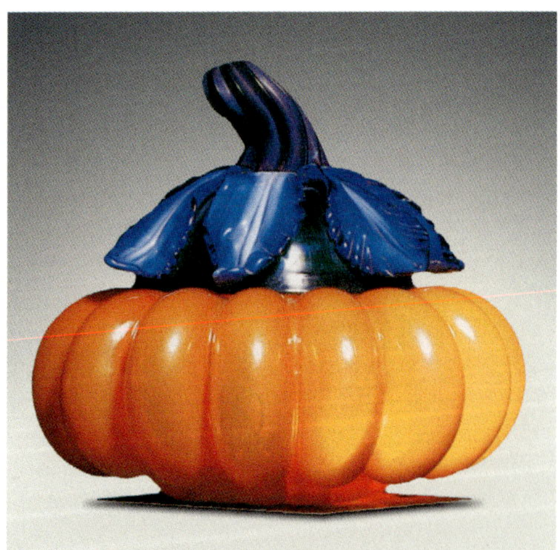

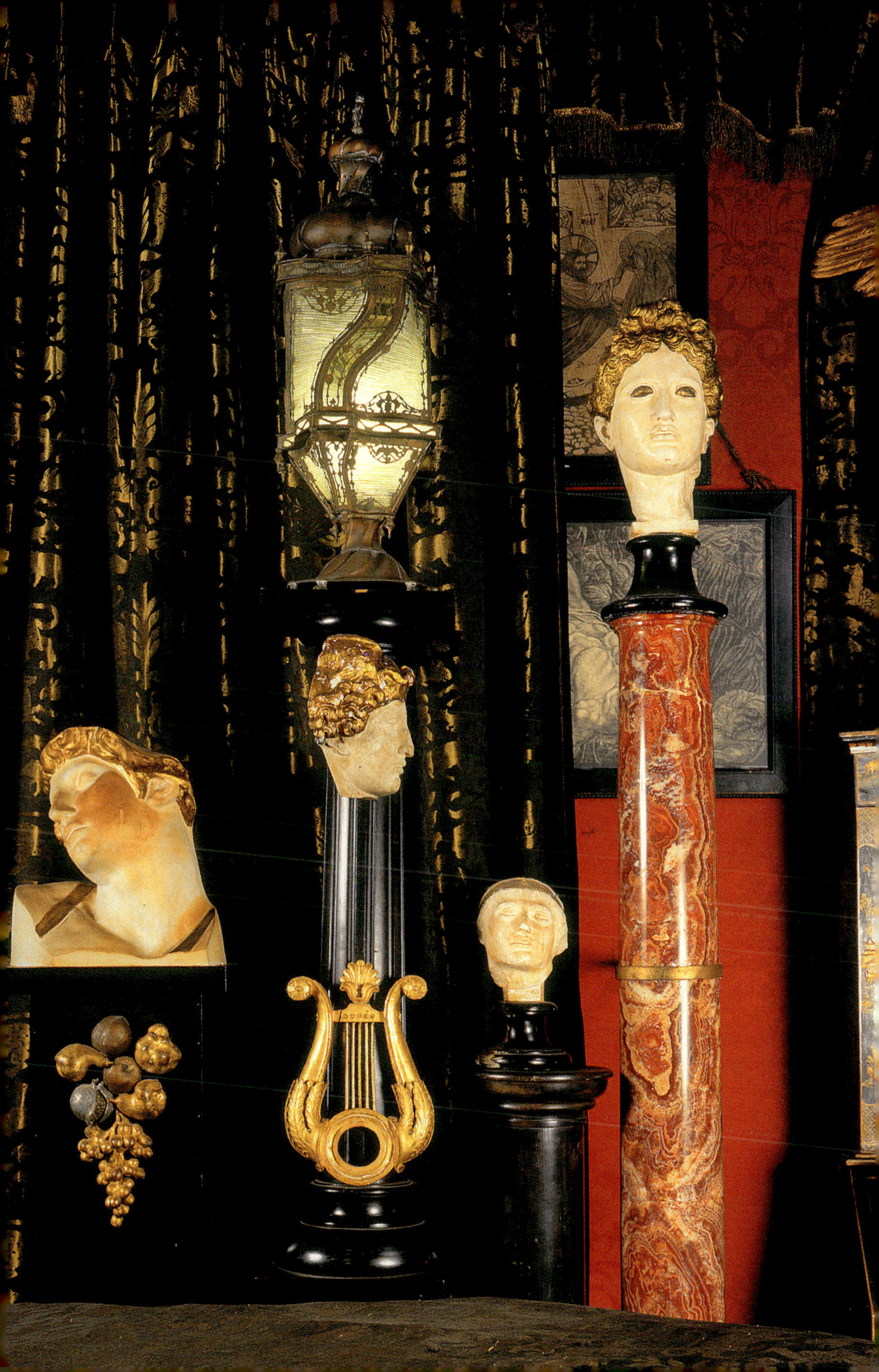

Marcel-André Bouraine, *Diana the Huntress*

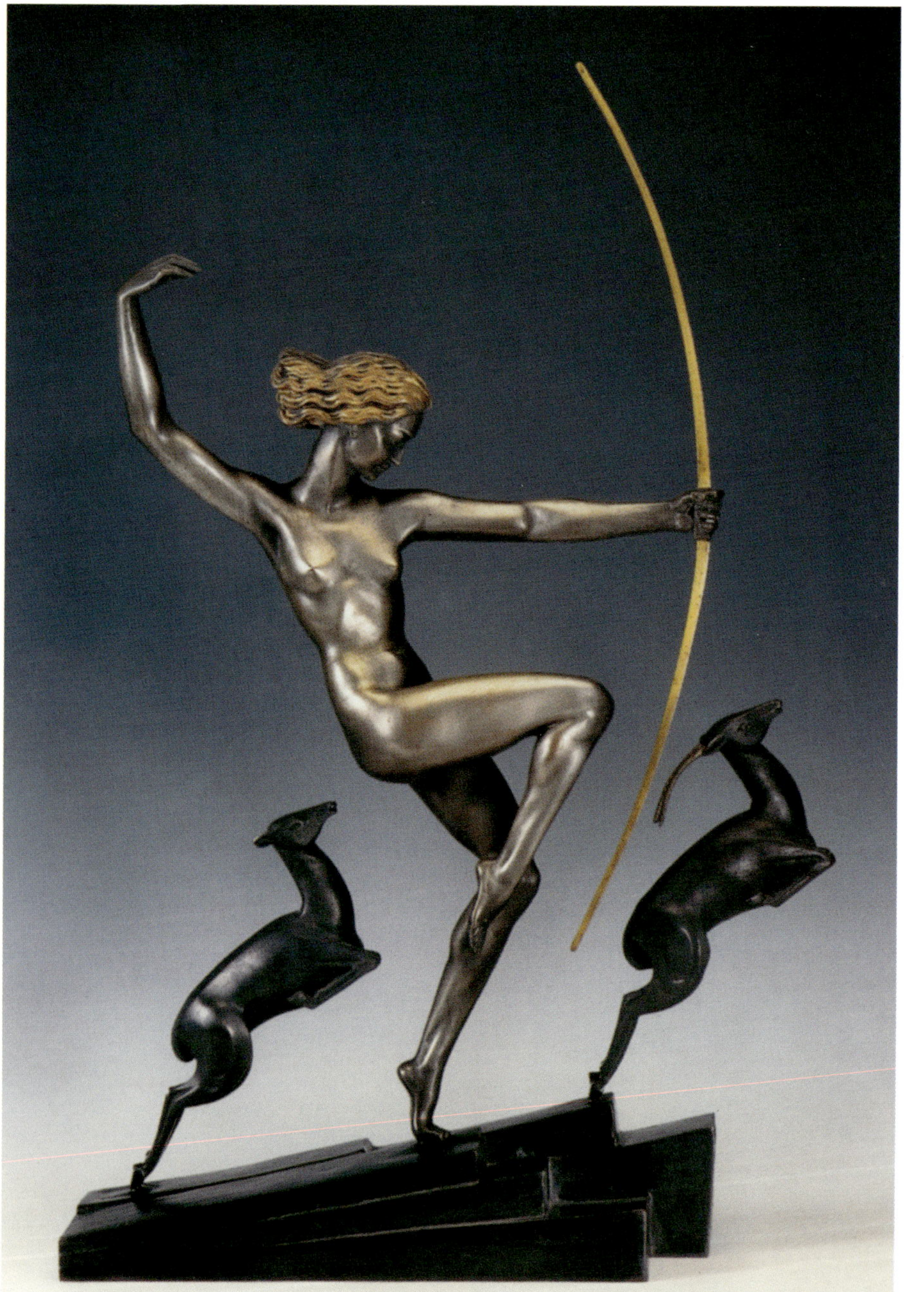

etry began with 200 verses by Dante and – after a long interval – it is continuing with me."

At the corner of the southern wall, is the gold plaster wing of *Victory in the air* by Renato Brozzi, with the bronze head from the same work resting on the top of a column, previously having been in the *Arengo*. The fireplace, designed by Maroni with polychrome marble columns, displays the motto which d'Annunzio had at La Capponcina: "Chi l'tenerà legato?" ("Who will keep it bound?"). Every space eventually came to be filled with furniture in Chinese style, divans, two grand pianos, small tables, bronzes, musical instruments, a holy water stoup in the form of a lotus flower, plaster casts of classical works (including a gilded and bejewelled *Kouros*, an *Aphrodite*, and a *Hermes*, the inventor of the lyre according to Greek mythology), Buddhas, Chinese dragons, the bronze of *Diana the Huntress* by Marcel-André Bouraine, a *Centaur archer* by Napoleone Martinuzzi, a gilded plaster cast representing *Leda loved by Zeus* in the form of a swan, an *Apollo musagetes*, the head of Michelangelo's *Dying Prisoner* (gilded by d'Annunzio), and plaster casts of the faces of Liszt and Wagner.

The numerous animals in the room – bronze serpents, a rhinoceros, Foo dogs – together with the room's musical references, recall the Orpheus myth, and the role of music as a civilizing power. The *Carta del Carnaro*, the constitution produced by "commandant" d'Annunzio during the Regency over Fiume (8 September 1920) in which he affirms Fiume's Italian essence and considers founding a revolutionary and corporate state, declares: "In the Italian Regency of Carnaro, Music is a religious and social institution. [...] if every new order is a lyrical order in the vigorous and impetuous sense of the word, Music, considered as a ritual language, exalts the act of life, the work of life."

It was from the first window on the right that d'Annunzio fell, on the evening of 13 August 1922, in circumstances that have never been clear – in what has been called the "flight of the angel". The "flight" of three metres eighty centimetres caused the "archangel" to fracture his skull and led to concussion of the brain. There have been many suppositions about what happened, but the most likely is that while Luisa Baccara was playing the piano, her younger sister, Jolanda, called affectionately Joiò, was trying to repel the poet's advances as he importuned her sitting astride the windowsill, and that she pushed him away too forcefully, making him lose his balance. From the delirium of the next few days – the poet remained in bed unconscious or semi-conscious for a fortnight – a fantastic and poetic "diary" was collected and transcribed by his two trusted doctors, his friend Antonio Duse (no relation of Eleonora) and Francesco D'Agostino, which was published in the *Comento meditato a un discorso improvviso* (*A meditated comment on an improvised speech*) included in the *Libro ascetico della giovane Italia* (*Ascetic book of the young Italy*) (1926), and more recently in a critics' edition (1995) with the title *Siamo spiriti azzurri e stelle (We are blue spirits and stars)*.

Many have claimed that had that fall not happened, the history of Italy might have been different: in fact, a meeting had been arranged for three days later, two months after the March on Rome, between d'Annunzio, Mussolini, who had supported the Fiume adventure and who looked up to d'Annunzio as a protective god, and Francesco Nitti, former President of the Council; the aim, in that period of social disorder and strikes, was to draw up a political plan that would lead to a government with widespread support, united against the left.

Stanza del Mappamondo (Room of the Globe)

This room was Thode's library, a spacious room with walls covered in plain dark wooden shelves, still holding many of the volumes that belonged to the German art historian. So it was a library, but also the dining room (especially when there were special dinners with the publishers, first Treves and later Mondadori), and it was also a "sacrarium" – a place of historical memories. Some Napoleonic memorabilia has been collected here: Napoleon's funeral mask, placed on a travertine high relief depicting an eagle, the snuff box he used on St Helena by the ex-Emperor, a gift from a Fiume legionnaire, the imperial seal in silver and agate engraved with an Egyptian sphinx, and a copy of the *Mémorial de Saint-Hélène* by Las Cases; all these objects were dear to the poet and are described at length in the pages of the *Libro segreto*.

On the walls and shelves, great artists and masterpieces of the past are evoked through plaster copies: the *Saint Teresa* by Gian Lorenzo Bernini, the *Pitti Tondo* and the hand of Michelangelo's David (there is also a plaster cast of the portrait of the great artist), two fifteenth century

Room
of the Globe

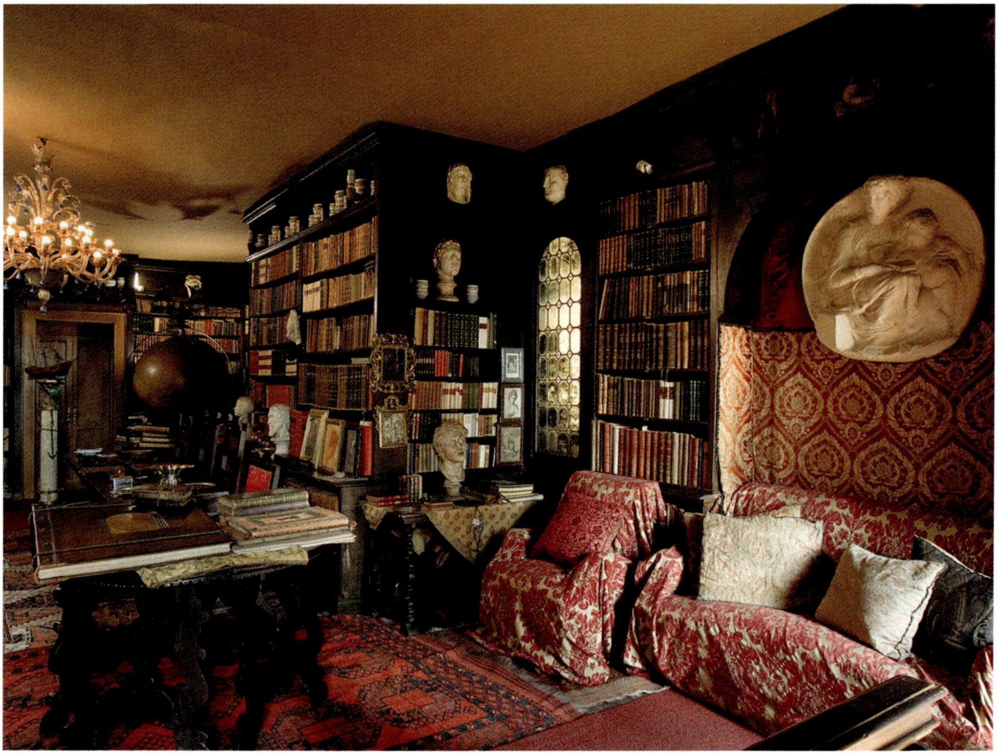

portraits – one of *Beatrice d'Aragon*) by the Dalmatian sculptor and architect Luciano Laurana. The great woodcut of *Dantes Adriaticus* by Adolfo De Carolis stands in a niche. On the small round table is an enormous copy of the *Divina Commedia* (*Inferno*) illustrated by the Genovese painter Amos Nattini, produced in 1921 for the sixth centenary of Dante's death.
A large world globe dominates the room, mounted on a base, on which d'Annunzio had a wrought iron galleon placed; written on a pennant in Venetian dialect are the words: "Strensé el mondo e slarghè la Dominante. El Dose" ("To hold tight the world and to enlarge the Dominant [Venice]. The Doge"). Another small wooden ship stands on a nearby marble column, while a large model of a Venetian galley, also used as a lamp, is attached to the eastern wall, above the organ (framed by shelves designed by Maroni) which was sometimes played by Luisa Baccara. On the internal shelves of the organ are eight plaster statuettes depicting mourning monks.
On the architrave above the door leading to the *Gamma corridor*, towards the *Stanza delle Reliquie*, there is a motto with words by the monk and doctor of the church, Bernardo di Chiaravalle: "Aliquid amplius invenies in silvis quam in libris" ("You will find more in woods than in books"). It is the same phrase that is carved on the elegant card catalogue of the Vittoriale Library.

Zambracca

This beautiful, delightful room, the "zambra" (which in Provencal dialect means bedroom, and also slovenly and untidy serving woman), was a cloakroom (the three wardrobes still contain some clothes), an intimate private study, and also a dining room for quick solitary meals. The walls are covered with green damask tapestries, while the wardrobe doors show the Monte Nevoso coat of arms

Zambracca

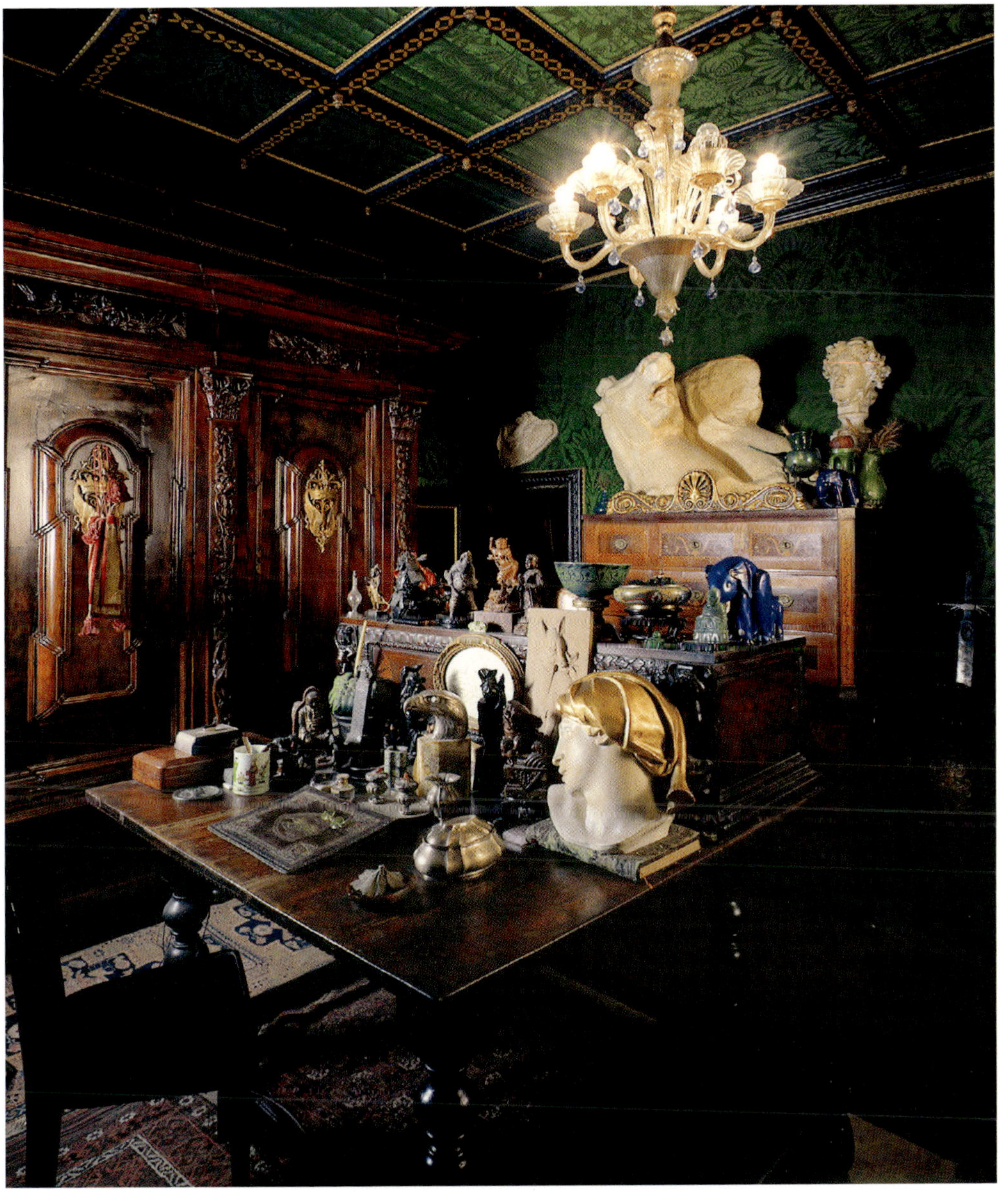

Renato Brozzi,
Panther

Alessandro Mazzucottelli,
Fireguard

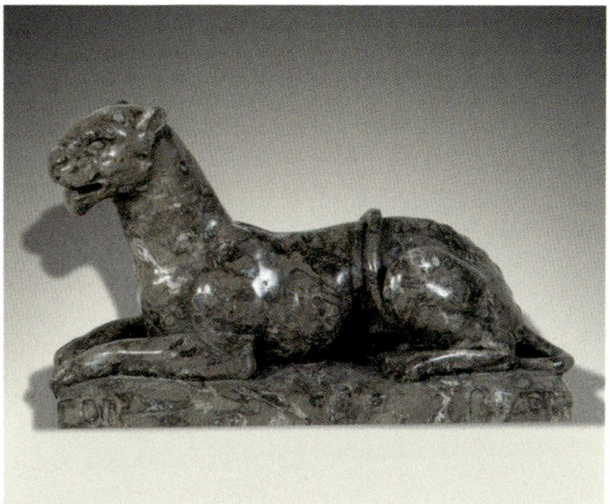

in bronze (the anchor with two wings and the prince's crown), and the room is dominated by some plaster casts: the cast of the head from Michelangelo's *Aurora*, the whole cast of which is in the Schifamondo, and the "sublime mutilated horses of Helios" as the poet called them, plaster casts of the Phidias horses from the Parthenon.
On the writing desk there is a writing set with a silver pen by the gold and silversmith Mario Buccellati, whom the poet called "Master Paragon Coppella", founder of the Buccellati jewellery shop in Milan, a favourite among the international aristocracy since the 1920s, together with an eagle's head, also in silver, with two precious stones for eyes, made by the expert "animaliere" ("animal sculptor") Renato Brozzi, whom Gabriele described in his *Libro segreto* as "descended from Pisanello". Also by Brozzi is the grey marble panther placed between the windows. There are also some Chinese sculptures on the desk (a bronze tortoise from the eighteenth century), silverware, pieces of Japanese porcelain, crafted leather and a large green piece of malachite. In the wooden niches in the walls on the garden side, and scattered around the room, are fine glass and porcelain objects. Napoleone Martinuzzi made the vase in Pulegoso glass with golden handles (the Murano glass master-craftsman created it using a particular technique that incorporates irregular bubbles of air within the glass paste, creating a special "frothy" effect), as well as the glass elephants and tapir on the desk and chest of drawers.
Gabriele d'Annunzio was sitting at this writing desk when he died of a cerebral haemorrhage on the evening of 1 March 1938, a cold, grey, rainy day, as the records inform us.

Stanza della Leda (Leda Room)

The architrave of the entrance door is inscribed with the words: "Genio et Voluptati" ("To Genius and Pleasure"); while the corresponding one on the opposite side has a copy of a tile from the apartment of Isabella d'Este, in the Palazzo Ducale in Mantova, with an imprint of the Sun and the motto "Per un dixir" ("For just one desire"). On the wooden beams of the ceiling, carved by Guido Marussig, are verses from Dante's *Rime*: "Three women have come round my heart / And sit outside it / For within sits Love / who holds sway over my life... ."
Completed in 1925, the bedroom, evidently dedicated to the theme of love, was immersed in the dominant colours of gold and blue, and illuminated by light from the Veranda dell'Apollino. The room takes its name from the gold plaster cast – standing in a niche beside silver animals by Renato Brozzi, Lalique glassware and oriental bronzes – a copy of a Greek original showing the union of Leda and Jove, who, according to the myth, fell in love with the beautiful Greek princess and turned himself into a swan in order to possess her. But, in evidence of the constant game d'Annunzio played

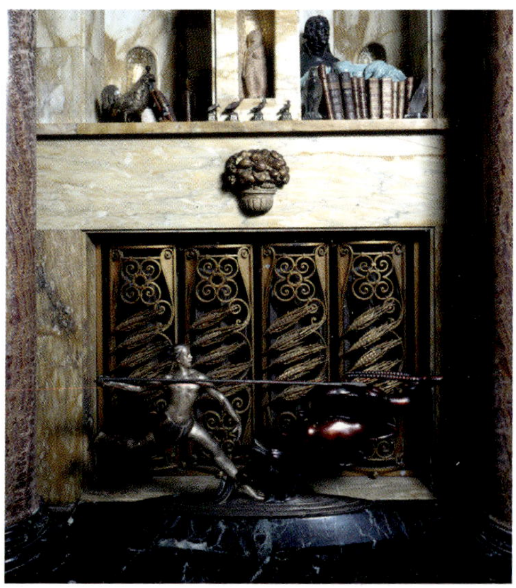

Leda Room

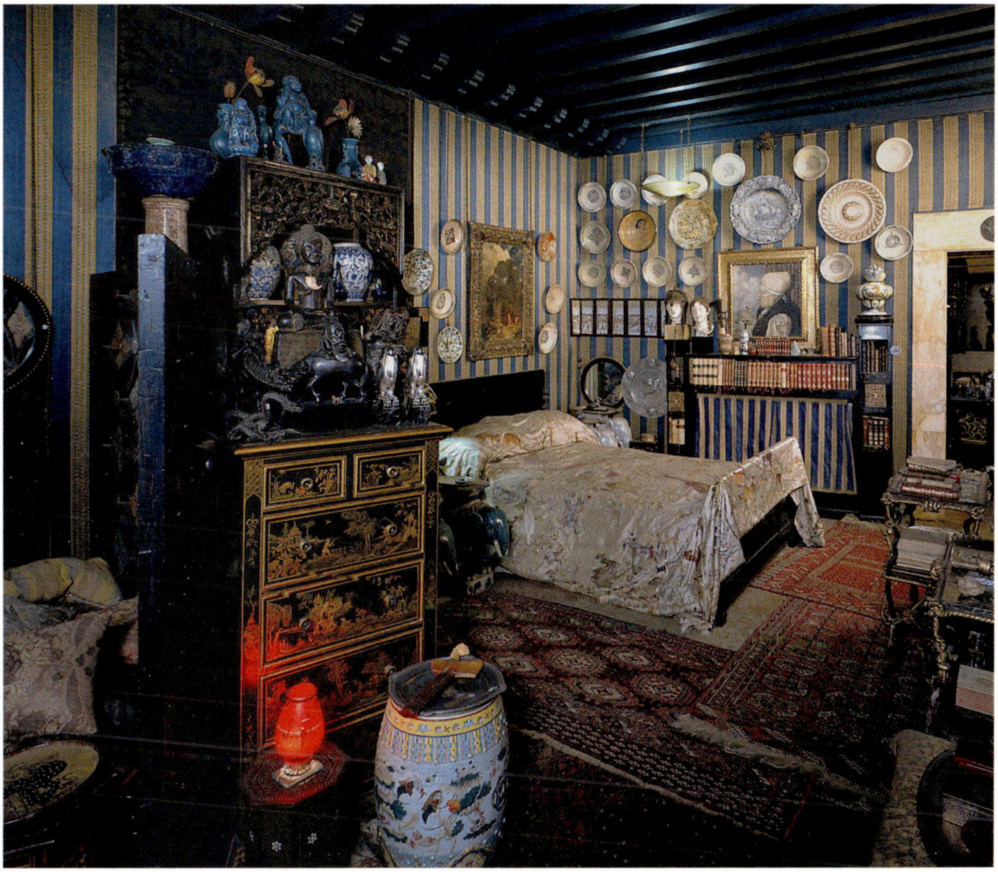

with the classical world and the past, *Leda senza cigno (Leda without the Swan)*, is also the title of one of d'Annunzio's novels published in 1913.
The fireplace is screened by a fireguard with decorations of wheat spikes made by Alessandro Mazzucottelli, a master craftsman of Milan Liberty-style wrought-ironwork from the late-nineteenth century to the early twentieth century, and collaborator of some of the greatest architects of the time. The three small double-top tables in green marble and iron Franciscan knotted cord, were designed by d'Annunzio himself.
Among the many western and oriental works of art is the plaster cast of Michelangelo's *Dying Prisoner*, standing on a wooden plinth with the inscription "Amor fati" ("love of destiny"); as d'Annunzio wrote in his *Libro segreto*, it is "the most beautiful and the saddest" of the group of six (four in the Gallerie dell'Accademia Florence and two in the Louvre), which the sculptor made as drafts for the unfinished tomb of Pope Julius II. Made in the workshops of the Louvre, and gilded and "clothed" by d'Annunzio himself (the brocade is fastened with a buckle forged by Martinuzzi), it was previously a feature of his residences at Capponcina and Arcachon. A Persian bedspread made of embroidered silk covers the bed, a gift from Maria Hardouin. Scattered around the room are Persian majolica ware, Chinese and Indonesian porcelain, six large elephants in Chinese majolica, also from his wife Maria, Spanish *azulejos*, enamels, gods, an

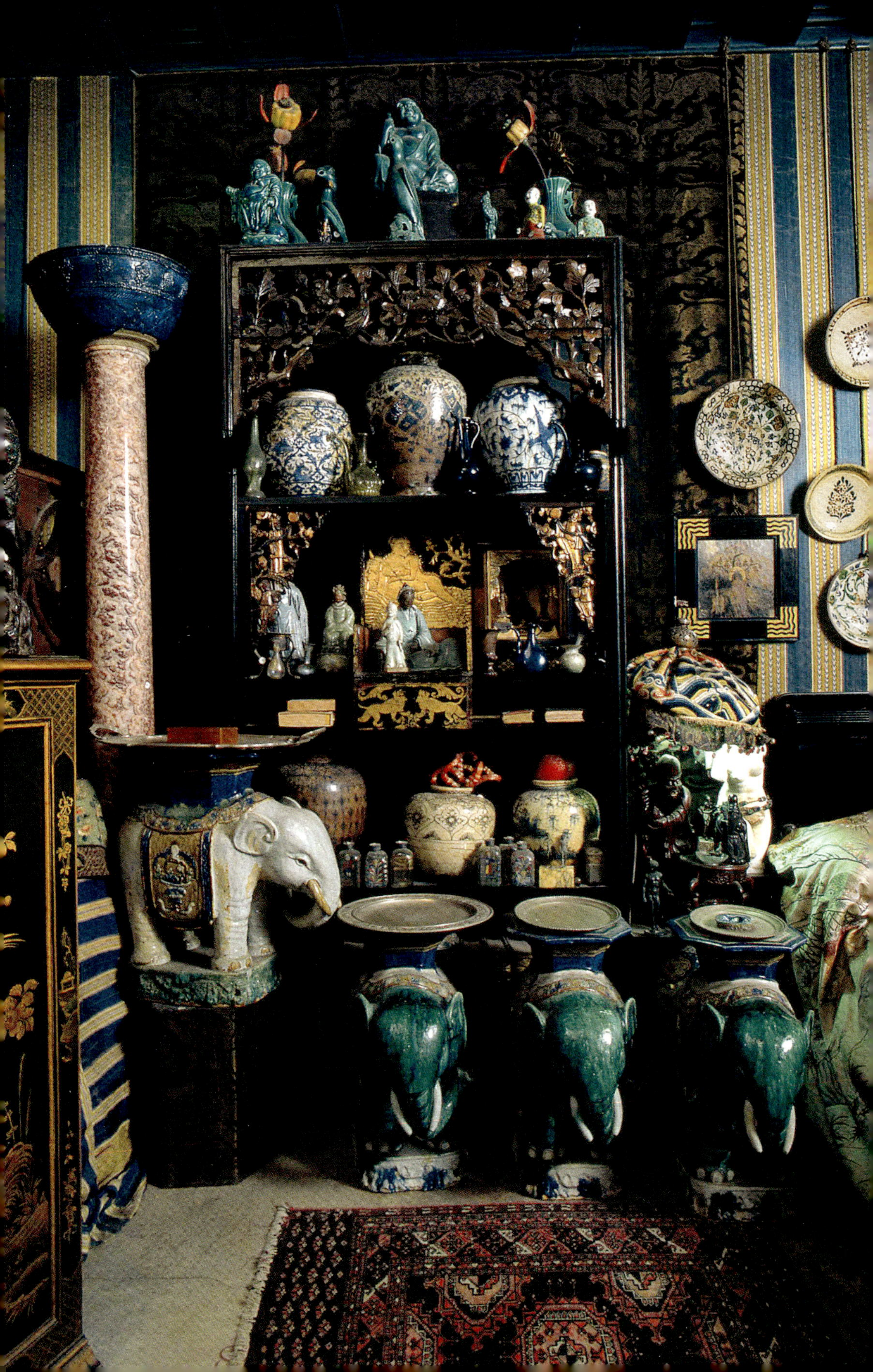

Leda Room

Plaster cast
of Michelangelo's
Dying Prisoner

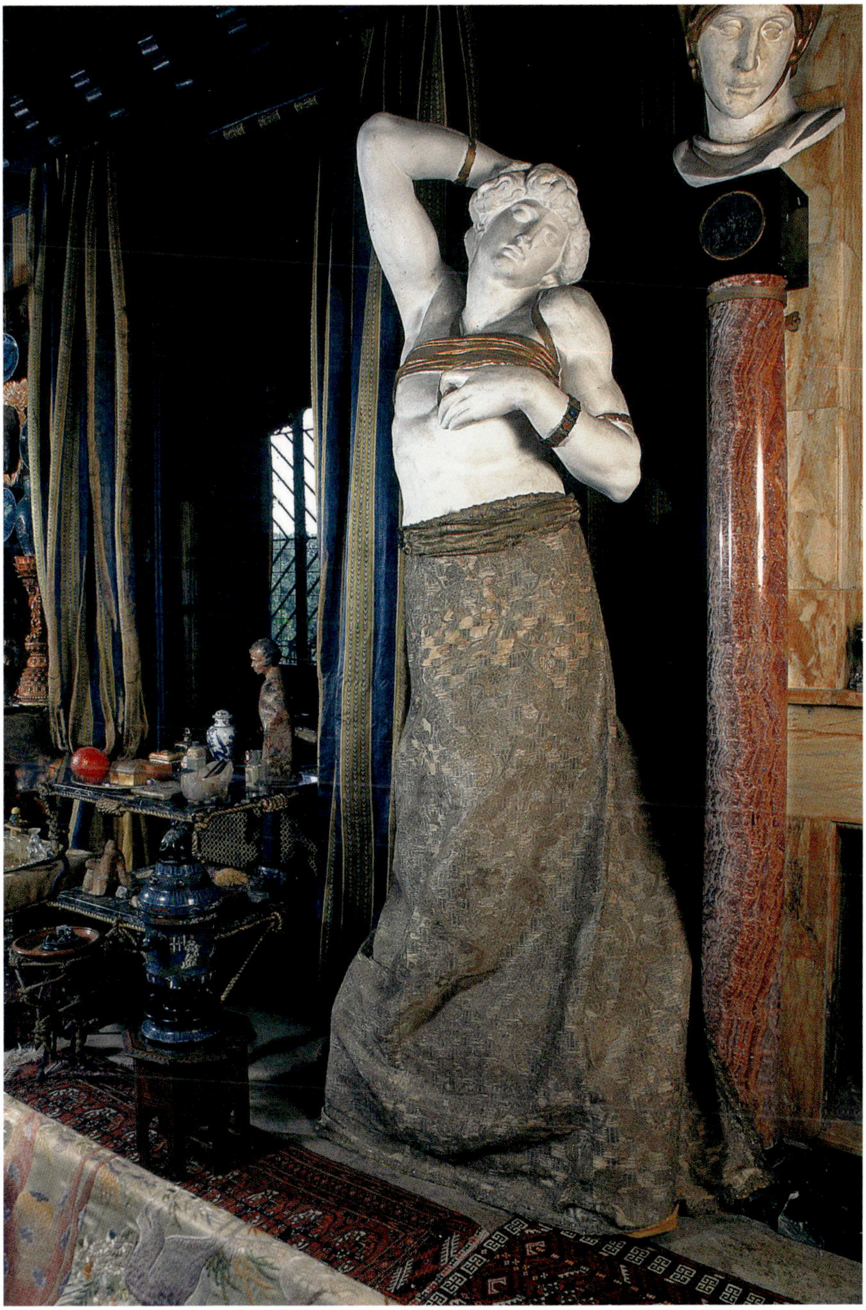

Veranda of the Apollino

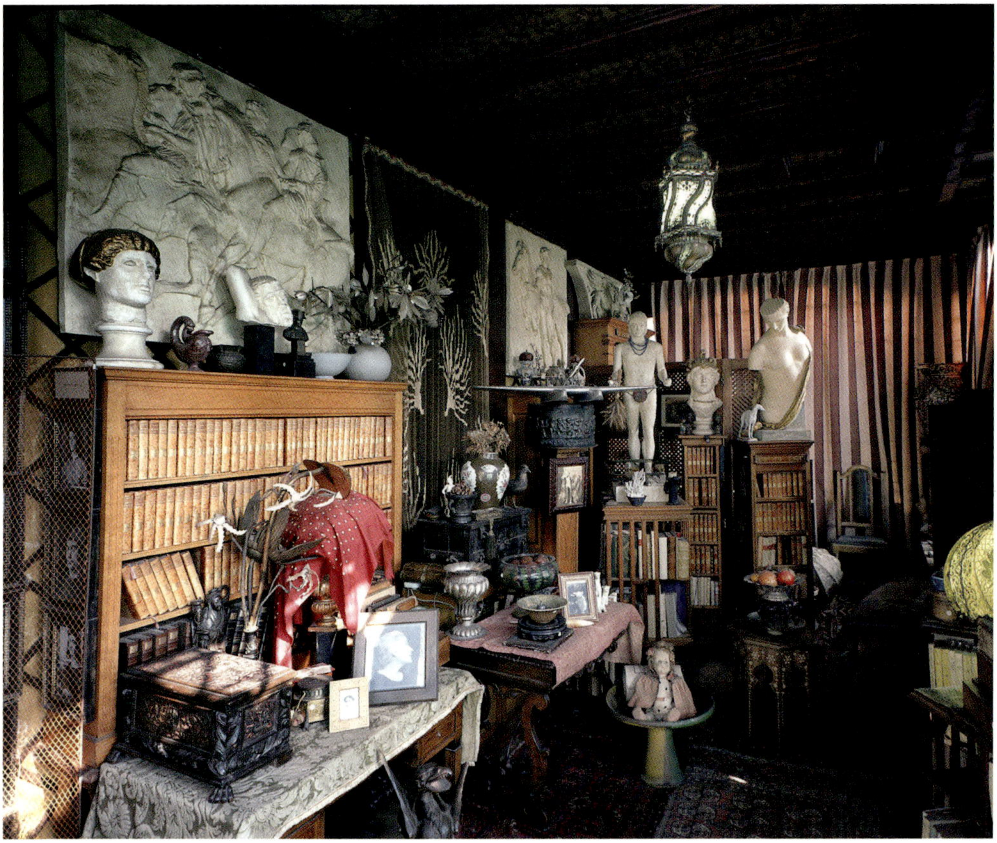

Egyptian funeral mask, and some modern ceramics by Fauna craftsman Pietro Meander. In keeping with the theme of sensuality and the union between men and women, which was also a common theme in his literature and in his life, with his insatiable desire for knowledge and pleasure, ("women are a science" he wrote in his notes, or again: "A force was given to me, harsh, savage, the frenzy of the male"), are the small silver and bronze sculptures by Renato Brozzi with priapic themes, and the small plaster *Aphrodite* beside the bed, adorned with a necklace of turquoise stones.

Three paintings hang on the walls: *Sinfonia. Après midi d'un faune*, by the symbolist artist Mario De Maria in 1909, inspired by the poem by Stéphane Mallarmé (1876), which also inspired the piece with the same name by Claude Debussy (1894). The artist's son, Astolfo De Maria, painted the *Allegoria erotica* (1917), and *La Dogaressa* (1917-1919), an allegory of old age inspired by the fifteenth century artist, d'Annunzio's fellow countryman, Gentile Bellini.

Veranda of the Apollino

This veranda was constructed by Maroni in order to filter light from the original façade of the villa into the bedroom, thus creating an intermediate environment that is bright and warm, suitable for relaxing and reading. The name comes from the plaster cast of an ancient Greek *Kouros*, previously at Arcachon, with blue eyes painted by d'Annunzio, who also added a spiked band around the wrist, and decorated it with a fabric loincloth and

The plaster cast of the Archaic *Kouros* which the veranda is named after

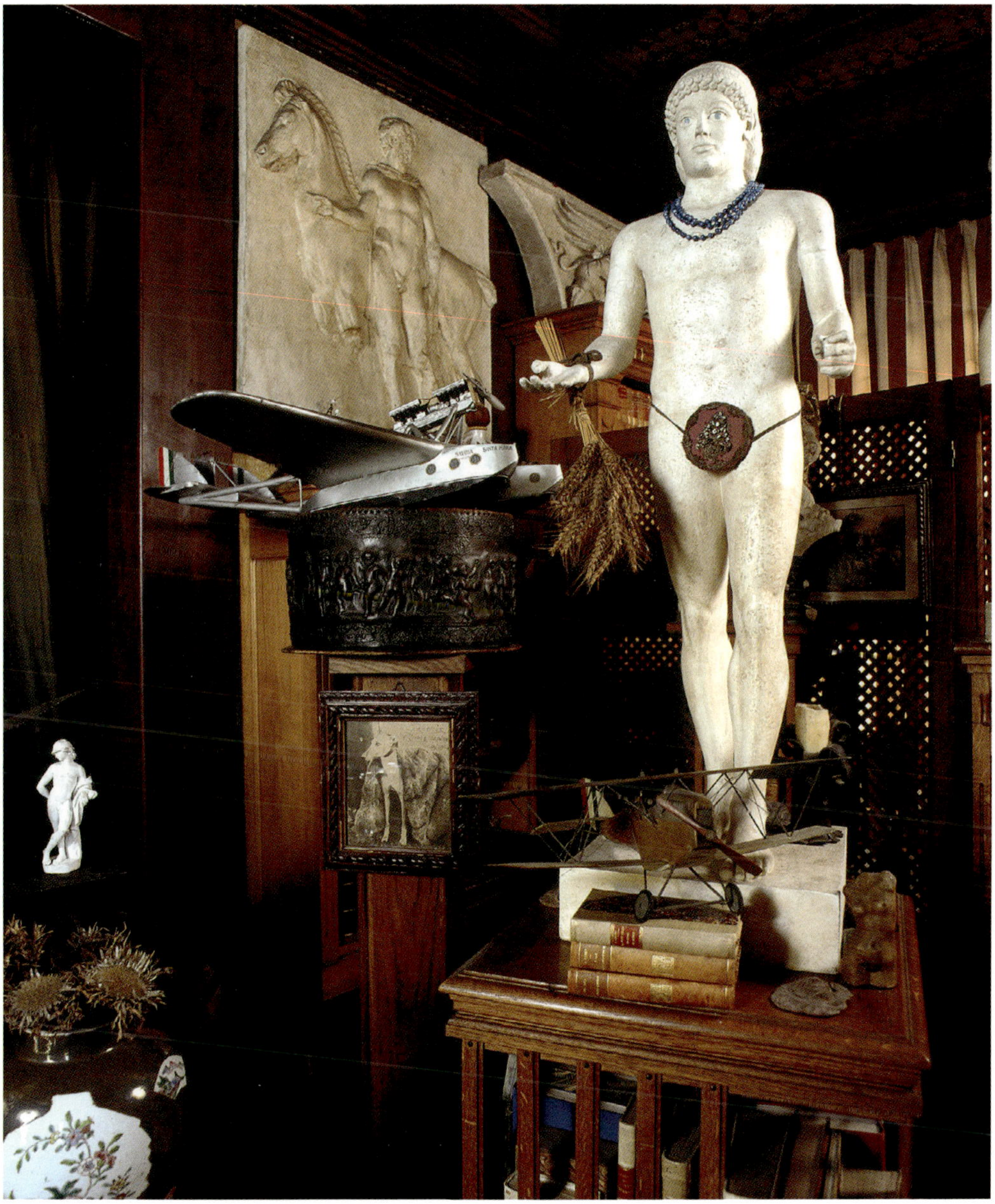

Blue Bathroom

Pietro Chiesa, *Stained-glass of the heron*

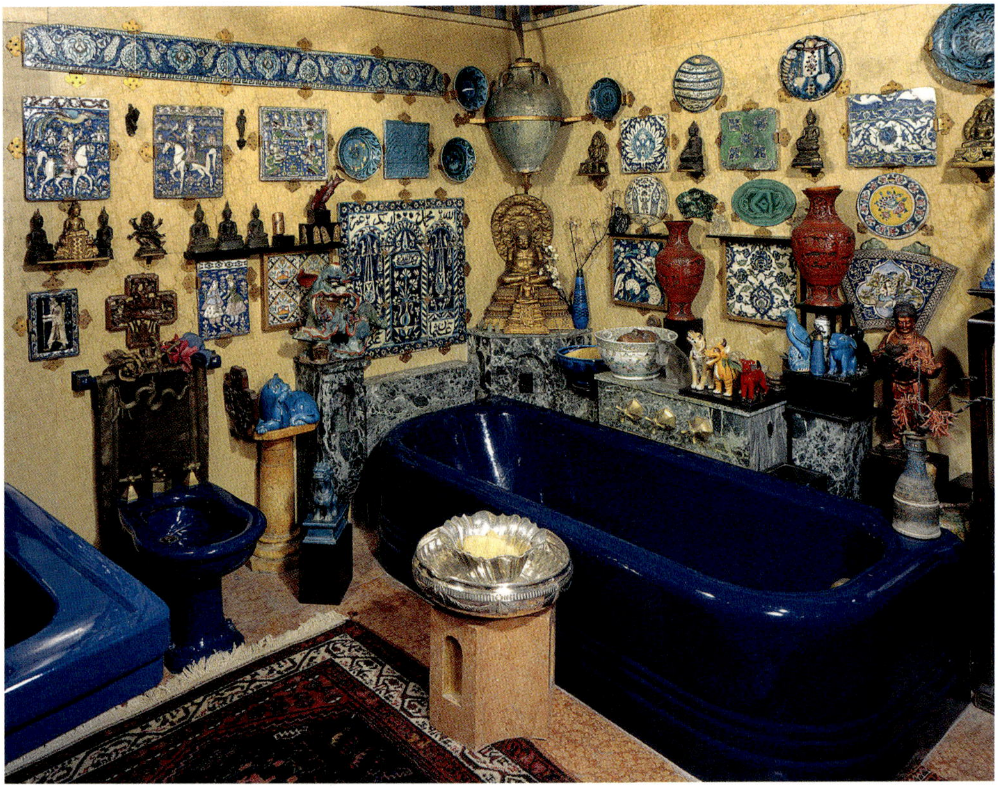

lapis lazuli stones and necklaces. Beside it is the cast of the *Psyche of Capua*; other casts from the Parthenon *Metopes*, are inserted in the walls. On the tables, shelves, and light oak swivel bookcases, in addition to books, there are numerous miniature animals, glass fruit, vases, cups, mother-of-pearl flowers, and photographic portraits of Gabriele's mother, Luisa, and of Eleonora Duse. Set into the doorposts are small reproductions of Renaissance masterpieces which belonged to Thode.

Bagno Blu (Blue Bathroom)

In 1931 the great architect and designer Gio Ponti was called on to work on the transformation of the kitchen and bathrooms of the Prioria, particularly the master bathroom, later called the "Blue Bathroom". Ponti was the founder, in 1928, of "Domus" magazine, which d'Annunzio knew so well that many of the objects published in its pages are to be found scattered around the rooms of the Vittoriale, and he upheld in his work and through his many different activities, the importance of a modern artistic craftsmanship, of high quality but accessible, with freshness in the forms and decoration. Thus, in this room of pleasure, which was certainly not simply a "utility room" (d'Annunzio always took great care of his own body, loved perfumes and created them himself), we find elegant blue bathroom fixtures designed by Ponti, with essential, modern shapes, and some of his artistic creations (a vase and a gilded ceramic bowl, for example), but mixed with a surprising number of objects for such a small space, all of them selected exclusively by the master of the house. On the walls, the surfaces, and the floor in pink Verona broccatello marble covered with oriental rugs, there are about eight hundred and fifty objects, including ceramics, glassware, statuettes, plaster

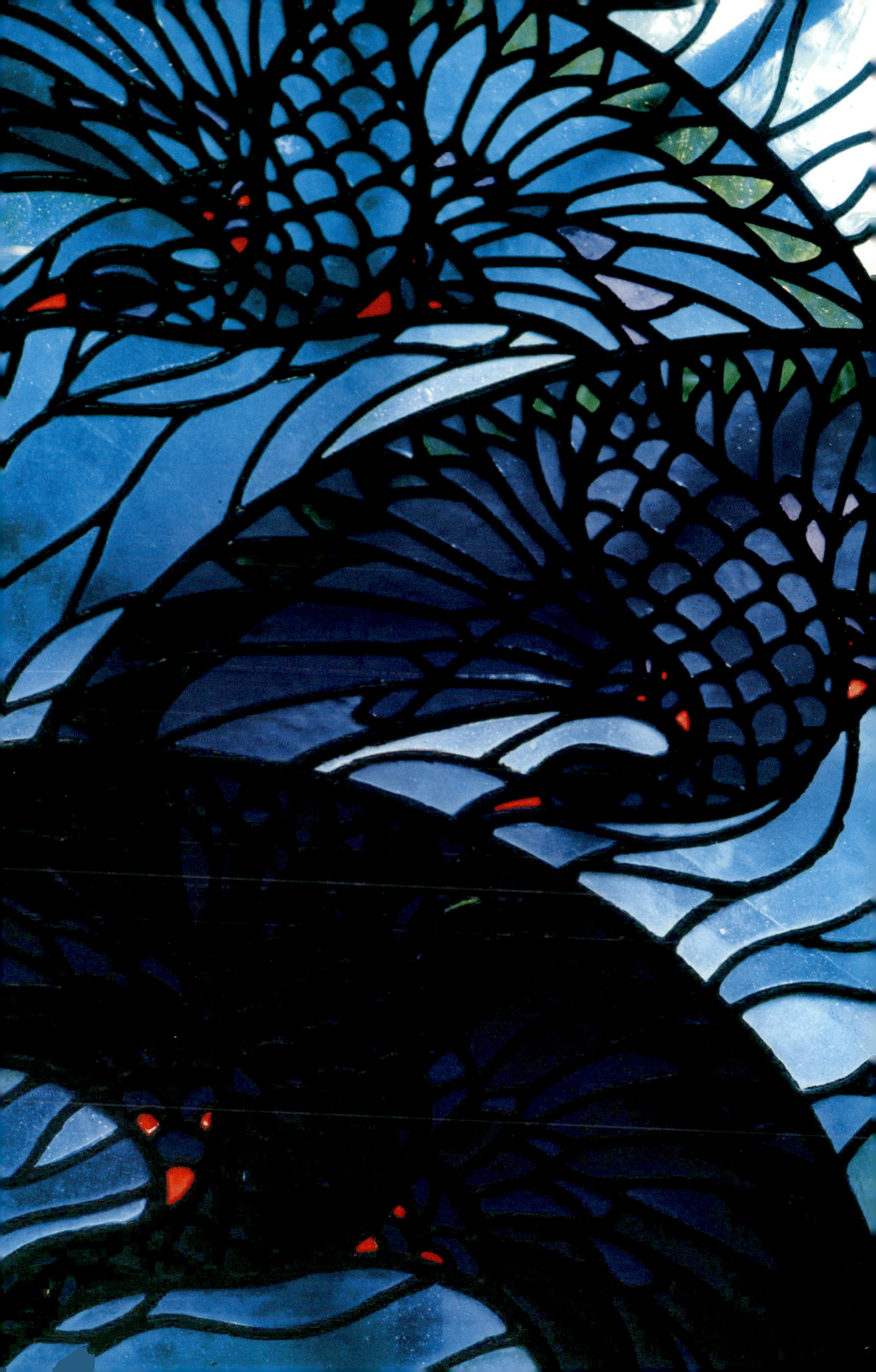

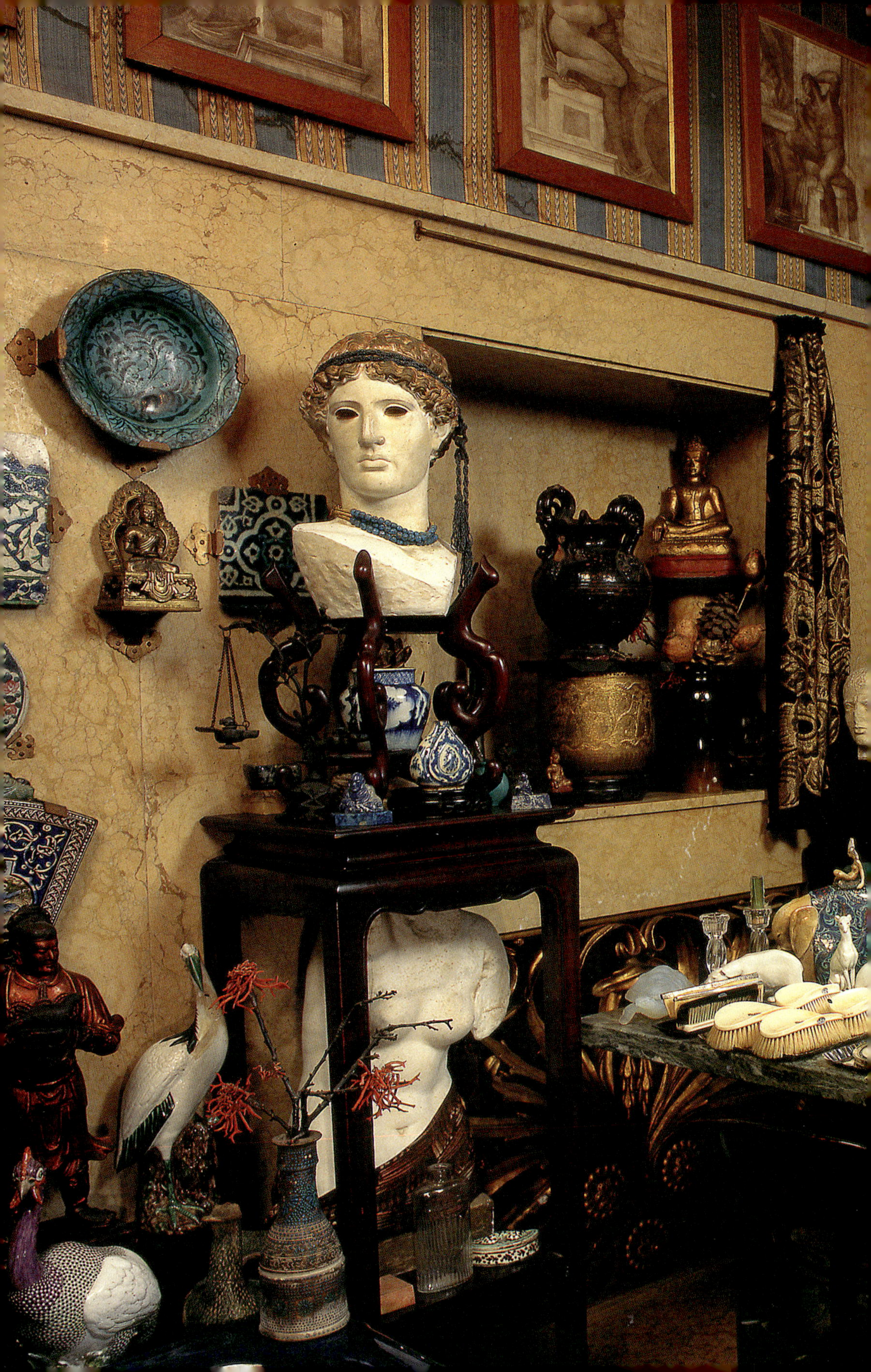

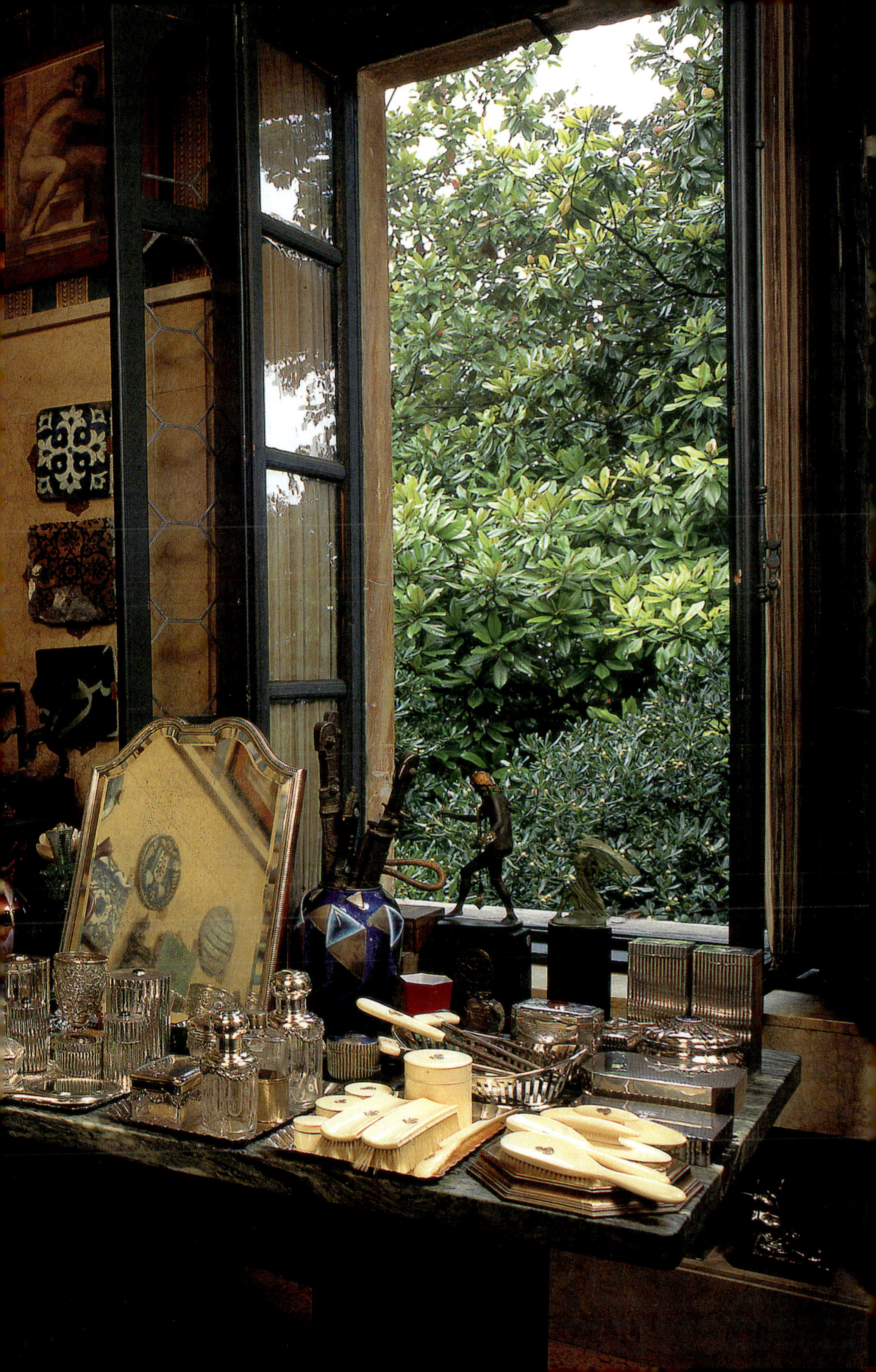

Francesco Nonni,
Bajadera

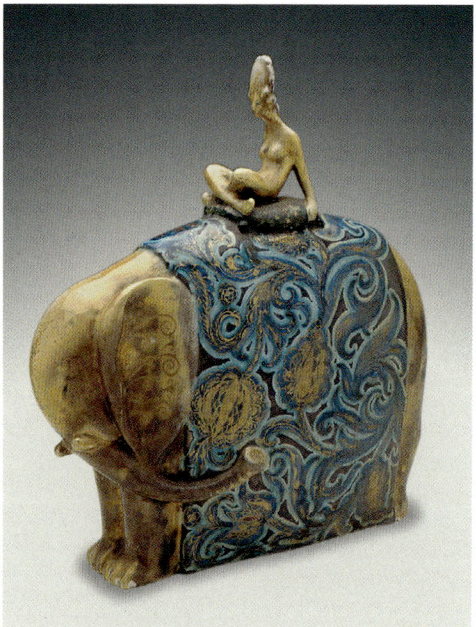

casts, bronzes, ewers, bottles, toilet tables, and animals of all kinds, in a very personal *horror vacui*, a long way from the rationalist trends that dominated Italian furnishings in the Thirties.
As in the other environments in the Prioria, there is an obvious desire to mix different cultures and epochs: together with the copy of Phidias's *Athena Lemnia* there is Arabic calligraphy, Persian ceramics, oriental bronzes, the little blown glass *Gazelle* by Martinuzzi, the *Bajadera on the elephant* by Faenza ceramics artist Francesco Nonni (repetition of the central part of the magnificent 1925 table centrepiece showing an *Oriental court*), and silverware by Mario Buccellati of the neo-eighteenth century graces, all exemplifying an elegant but highly varied twentieth century taste.
The coffered ceiling has a repeated motto painted by Guido Marussig, taken from the first *Olympian* ode by the Greek poet Pindar: "Water is the best of all". Hanging in the small passageway leading to the lavatory is a valuable tapestry in wool on jute dating from about 1916 and depicting warriors with swords and shields, by the Venice artist Vittorio Zecchin of 1919. The lavatory is finished with blue panelling and decorated with "horrifying" Japanese theatrical masks, as the poet called them, as well as two Rosenthal Art Déco heads, and the blue and navy "heron stained glass" by Pietro Chiesa.

Stanza del Lebbroso (Room of the Leper)

On 10 June 1924, Giacomo Matteotti was kidnapped and assassinated; but even before this d'Annunzio had been withdrawing more and more from political life, ever since the March on Rome – becoming like a leper, an outcast, a "reclusive scribe". "The early Christians honoured lepers as confessors of the faith. I am a leper and confessor", wrote the poet in one of his numerous notes.
It was in this period, between 1924 and 1925, that a new room was added to the old Villa Thode (actually completed in 1929), the only entirely *Art Déco* room together with the *Stanza della Cheli*. This was the *Stanza del Lebbroso* (*leper*), or of the *Misello or Miserello*, or of the pure Dreams, designed to be a room for meditation (the poet withdrew here on the anniversary of the death of his mother Luisa, of Eleonora Duse, and of other friends) and the future funeral chamber: the area that was the most secret, private and dense with symbolism in the whole house.
The furnishings and decorations were entrusted to Guido Cadorin (the two paintings, one above the door, of *Christ and Mary Magdalene* and one above the bed, of *Saint Francis Embracing the Leper D'Annunzio*, the allegorical panels on the coffered ceiling and wardrobe, and the designs for the stained glass), Napoleone Martinuzzi (the lamps) and Pietro Chiesa (creator of the two polychrome stained glass windows depicting the *Psalms,* and the one known as *delle stelle e del cielo* [of stars and sky]); the room is hung with deerskin panels in "the primitive colour of the Franciscan habit", as the poet expressly requested. The furniture and cupboards were designed by Maroni. In 1934 an early sixteenth century wooden statue by a Marche school (from the church of San Domenico in Camerino) was placed in the room, depicting Saint Sebastian pierced with arrows. D'Annunzio was always attracted to this saint, who was martyred in Rome under the emperor Diocletian. During his period in Arcachon, in 1910, he wrote *Le martyre de Saint Sébastien* directly in French. It was set to music by Claude Debussy, with whom d'Annunzio had a relationship of great mutual esteem; starring the celebrated Russian dancer, Ida Rubin-

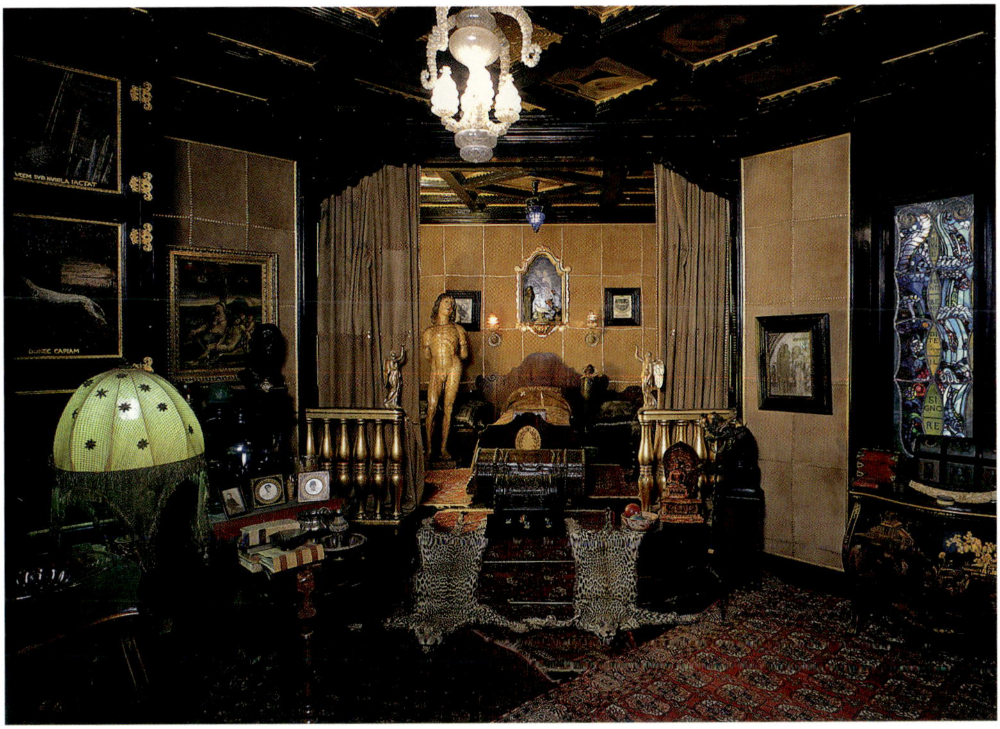

stein, and with costumes designed by Léon Bakst, the drama was staged in Paris in 1911. The day before the first performance, the archbishop of Paris declared that any Catholics who watched the performance would be excommunicated. The work was not very successful (Marcel Proust found it "pleasant but rather boring"), but public opinion was nevertheless scandalized by the fact that the role was given to a woman, and one who was the subject of much gossip, what is more, and because the play alluded to a homosexual relationship between Sebastian and the emperor. We also know, from d'Annunzio's own reminiscences, that as a young man, after a night of love which left him covered "with the marks of violent kisses" all over his body, he felt like a kind of "sensual" reincarnation of the saint, who is traditionally depicted pierced all over with arrows.

The iconographic arrangement of the room is complex, and it is not by chance that it was entrusted to Cadorin – whom d'Annunzio affectionately called "Fra Guidotto" – this refined Venetian artist was a member of the "secessionist" Cà Pesaro group and a friend of Napoleone Martinuzzi, and he lived with his family at the Vittoriale for the entire duration of the work. The ceiling panels, in between gilded plasterwork with symbols of Christ's passion, show five saints on wings, Sybil of Flanders, Elisabeth of Hungary, Odile of Alsace, Judith of Poland and Catherine of Siena, recalling the vision which the poet had during a visit to Ferrara, of a possible future life of isolation and monasticism, dedicated to love of beauty, which he describes in the *Faville del maglio* (1924). As his models for the faces of the five saints, Cadorin took Luisa Baccara (Saint Catherine), three of d'Annunzio's friends (Maria Cecilia Monteverde, Betty Lewis, and Beatrice Orsi Beuf) and Cadorin's own wife Livia (Saint Sybil). The beautiful charcoal preliminary sketches are preserved in the Villa archives. The panels on the corner cupboard are also by Cadorin and depict a nude woman (accompanied by the Motto "Semper non semper"), a

Pietro Chiesa,
*Stained -glass
of stars and sky*

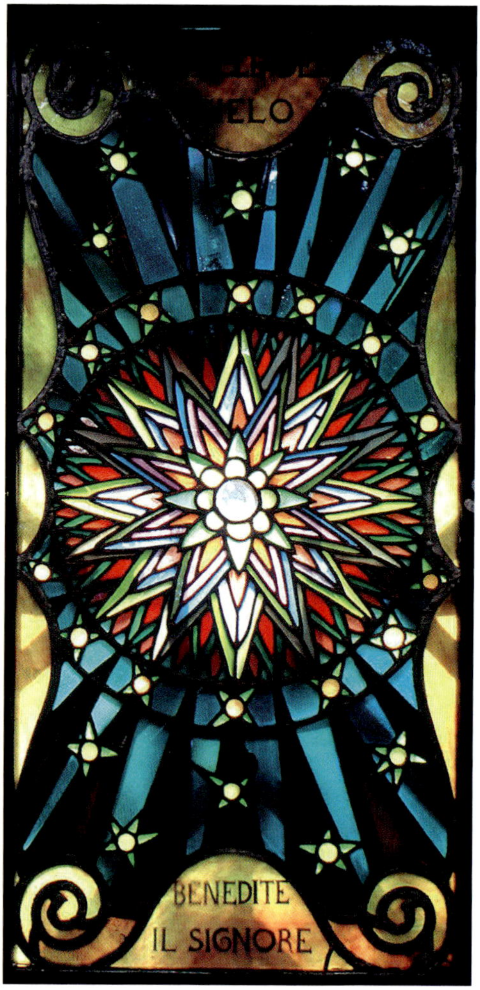

Vittorio Zecchin,
Vestal Globet

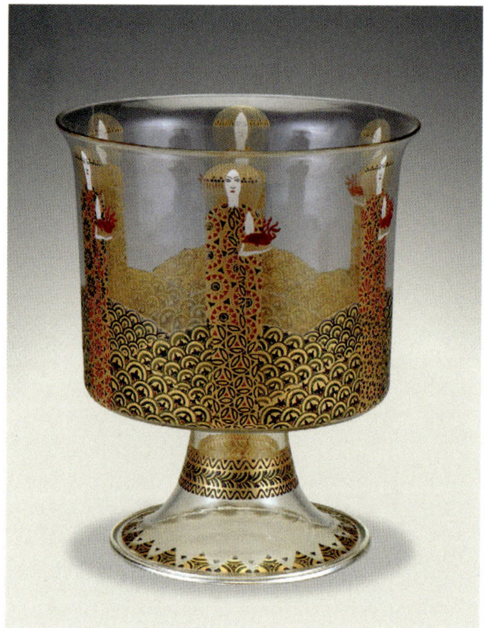

horse rearing on its hind legs ("Morsu praestantior"), a greyhound ("Donec capiam"), a seaplane ("non sufficit orbis"), unsheathed blades ("Lucem sub nubila jactat"), the D'Annunzian muse "Energeja" in the form of a woman archer drawing her bow ("fert diem et horam"), a bonfire ("Solus fortes terret ignis non me"), and an organ ("Numquam dissonis").

The bed, inspired by the sixteenth century Ravenna tomb of Guidarello Guidarelli, attributed to Tullio Lombardo, stands on a platform separated from the rest of the room by gilded wooden banisters with two angels. There is also a funeral mask of Guidarello, Cesare Borgia's noble, handsome *condottiero* who was the subject of a sonnet by d'Annunzio in 1903, on one of the two Chinese chests of drawers. "Half cradle, half coffin" is how d'Annunzio described the bed, which is covered with a suede bedspread with a design of a radiant sun, and the motto "Dona e non iscema". This was where the poet's coffin was displayed on the night between 1 and 2 March 1938. In the niche above the bed, in front of the *Saint Francis* by Cadorin, is a small bronze statue of the *Madonna of Peace*, donated by the symbolist sculptor Leonardo Bistolfi.

The panels in the ceiling above the bed contain inscriptions, all alluding to solitude and the rebirth connected to the spiritual life: "Prison I sing, Thus I live, thus I wound, Solitary and alone, Safe from rust, Burning I rise, As long as I am on high, I have fire with me for eternity".

On both sides of the bed are wardrobes against the wall, with images of the archangels and the four elements: "Michael" and "Gabriel" with "Air" (an aeroplane) and "Water" (two women washing themselves); on the right "Ariel" and "Raphael", with "Fire" (the fireplace) and

Room of the Leper,
alcove with the
wooden statue of
Saint Sebastian

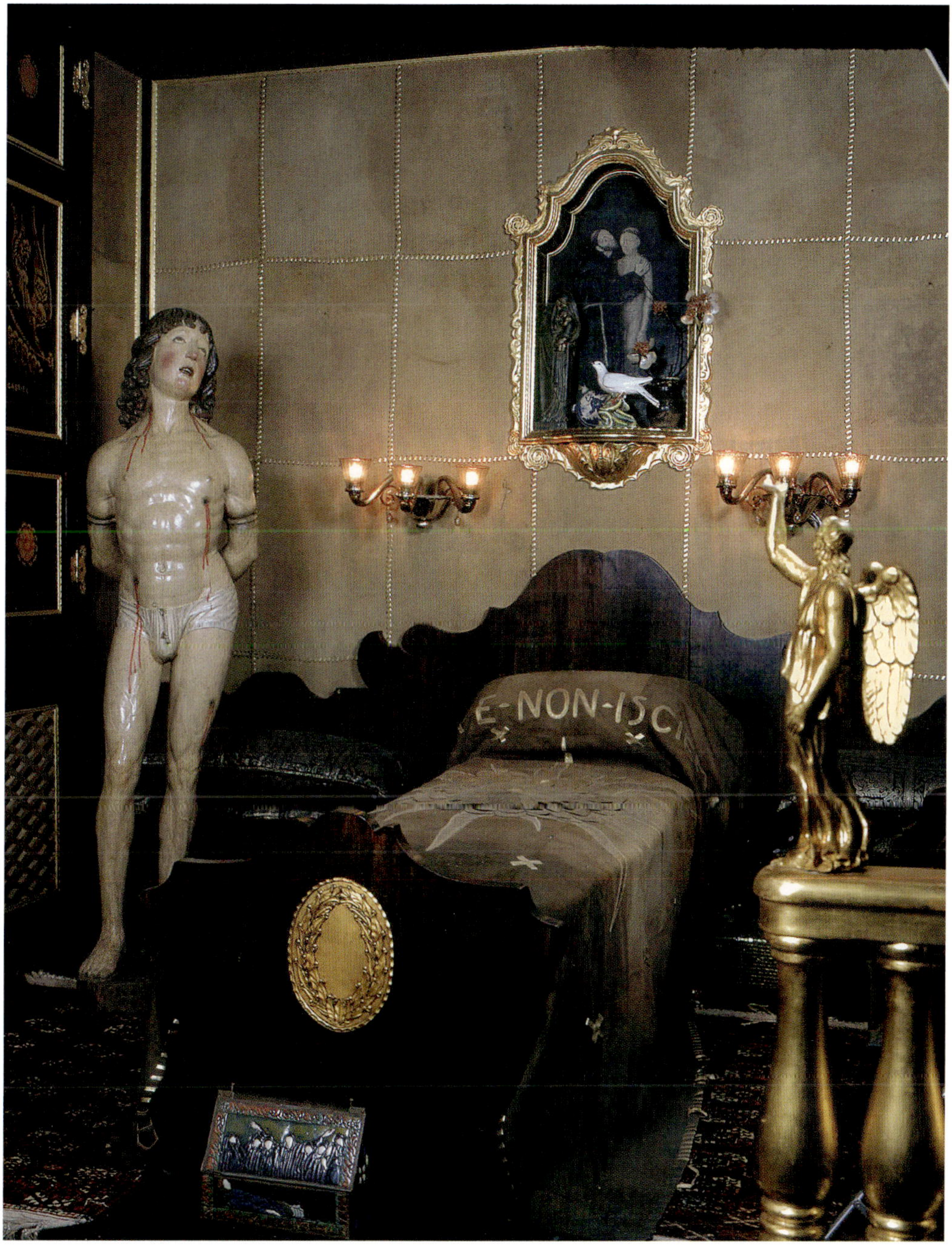

Pietro Chiesa,
Stained-glass of Saint Cecilia

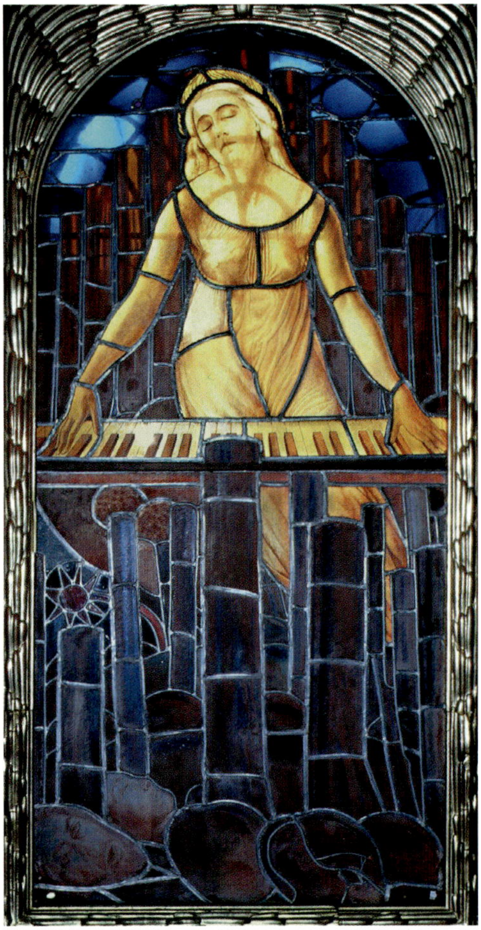

"Earth" (Eden). Scattered around the room are precious objects, full of meaning, such as the sixteenth century table with the *Pietà*, attributed to Spinello Aretino, the *Vestal Goblet* in blown transparent glass with polychrome enamel and gold – a work in secessionist style made in 1919 by the Venetian master Vittoro Zecchin, the plaster cast of the famous portrait of *Seneca*, and photographic portraits of Eleonora Duse, Luisa d'Annunzio and the poet's sister, Elvira.
Everything, the objects of art, the colours, the decorations, the mottos, serves to emphasize the atmosphere of solitude, spirituality, expectation and the foreshadowing of death. "The room is a miracle beyond your art and beyond my inspiration. It is a miracle and a mystery for both unknowables" the poet wrote to Cadorin, thanking him at the completion of the work for having understood so well the "spirit" of the room.

Corridoio della Via Crucis (Via Crucis Corridor)

Originally the gallery of Villa Thode, the corridor takes its name from the enamelled copper panels by Giuseppe Guidi, an artist whose religious subjects were much appreciated by d'Annunzio, showing the stations of the Cross on the road to Calvary. The walls are covered with "vair" fabric, imitating the black and white fur of the squirrel, used during Medieval times and produced by the Lisio company in Florence (it is also used in the Officina); the Franciscan motto "Pax et Bonum" is inscribed along the border, to which d'Annunzio, with his usual taste for puns and plays on words, added "Malum et Pax". A wooden gate with a radiant sun (the "sun door") separates the gallery from the interior parts of the Prioria. Just before the gate, there is a painted plaster cast of one of the so-called *Piagnoni* (*mourners*), one of the eight monks from around the tomb of the Burgundian nobleman Philippe Pot, a French work from the end of the fifteenth century now in the Louvre. The stained glass windows that were originally planned, to be entrusted to Pietro Chiesa, were never made. The gallery overlooks the Cortile degli Schiavoni, with the Monte Nevoso coat of arms, and the Portico del parente.

Stanza delle Reliquie (Room of the Relics)

Completed in 1929, this room was designed to house relics and artefacts from all religions. Although an atheist, d'Annunzio was strongly attracted to monastic and Franciscan spirituality, and was equally curious and interested, sometimes from a merely "aesthetic" point of view, in all the other different religions: "From the honest puritan to the negro worshipping fetishes, all the religious beliefs resemble each other and are of equal value. They differ only in their language," he writes in a note.
This room was the former dining room and music room, previously called "Cenacolo" or "Stanza del contrappunto" (Counterpoint Room), and it contained memorabilia from the Fiume enterprise and the First World War, some of which is now displayed in the War Museum in Schifamondo, in that intermingling of the

Room
of the Relics

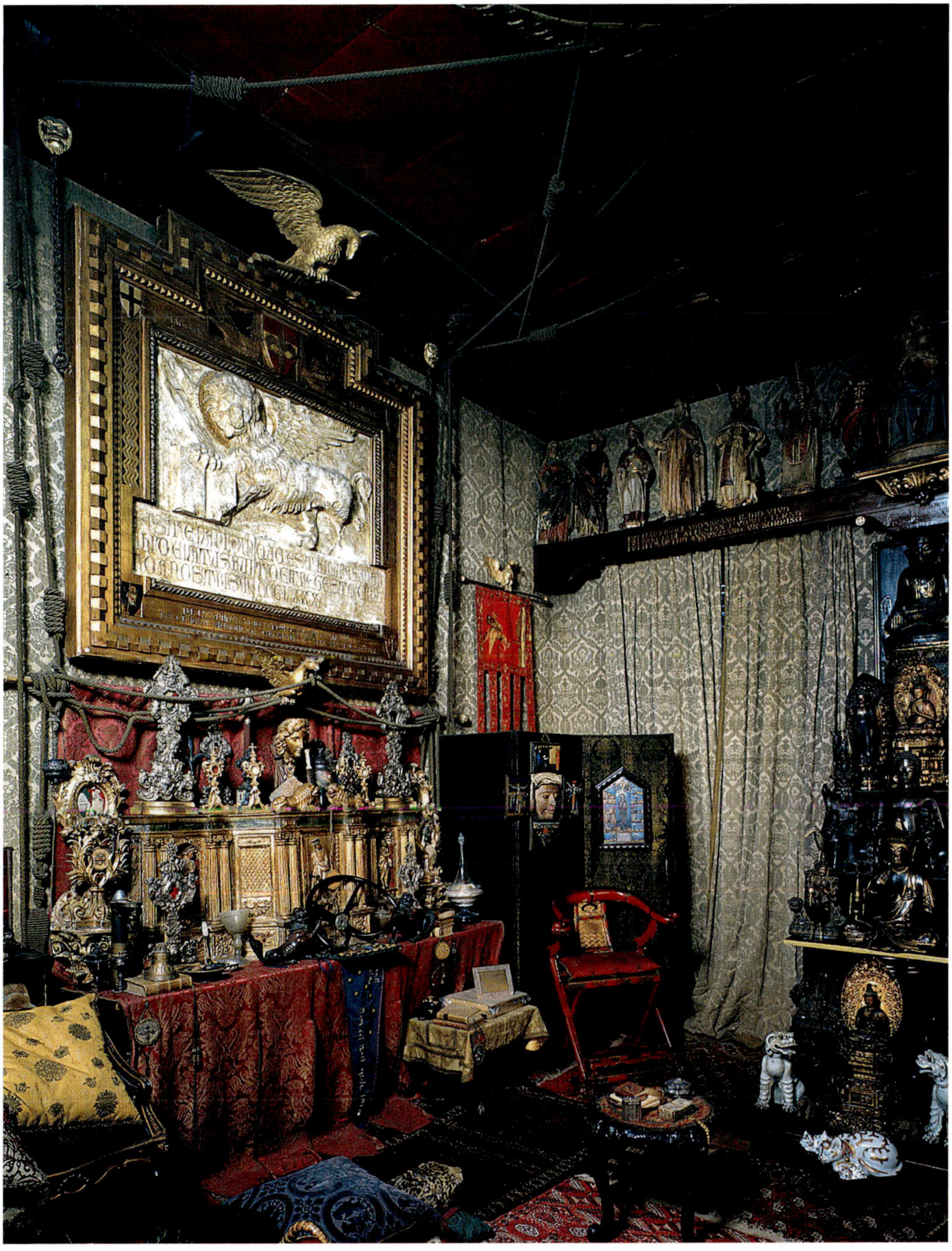

Napoleone Martinuzzi, set of Murano glass goblets

religious sacred with the military and patriotic sacred which was so typical of d'Annunzio. "A little while ago, in the salon of the Relics, among the Saints and Idols, the images of all beliefs, the aspects of all that is Divine, I was almost overwhelmed by the lyrical force of my religious synthesis," he wrote in 1935.

On the ceiling is the gonfalon of the Regency of Carnaro in red silk and gold thread, with, in the centre, the constellation of the Great Bear, the symbol of the serpent biting its tail (eternity) and the motto taken from St Paul's *Letter to the Romans*, "quis contra nos?" (in St Paul's letter it is preceded by the phrase "Si spiritus pro nobis"; "If God is for us, who can be against us?").

The sage-green printed cotton tapestries on the walls, with Franciscan cords creating lozenges between which roses alternate with pomegranates, were designed by Mariano Fortuny y Madrazo, whom d'Annunzio nicknamed "the alchemist dyer"; he was a refined artist of Catalan origin, active in Venice, and here, as well as painting, he produced clothing, fabrics and hangings with ornamental motifs inspired by medieval and classical themes.

A Flemish tapestry hangs from the beam, depicting a Biblical subject with figures showing the five fingers of a hand, and above them the motto "Cinque le dita, cinque le peccata" (Five fingers, five sins) — d'Annunzio excluded greed and lust from the seven deadly sins. Carved into the western wall is a bas-relief with the lion of Saint Mark, and the traditional inscription ("Pax tibi Marce..."), which was given to the poet by the city of Genoa on the occasion of his famous irredentist speech (5 May 1915) for the inauguration of the Monument to the Thousand by Eugenio Baroni.

The Lion of St Mark is also the subject of the painting by Guido Marussig on the left side of the same wall, this time depicted as the Lion of Victory ("Victoria tibi Marce..."), which previously hung in d'Annunzio's study in Fiume. Hit by a grenade fragment during the "Bloody Christmas" of 1920 (the fratricidal battle ordered by the Italian government which put an end to the Fiume adventure and the Regency of Carnaro), the painting still has the grenade splinter embedded in it, while the inscription beneath it reads: "Wounded in the left claw by a fragment shot by an Italian canon on the ship Andrea Doria, aimed at Italian Fiume against the Commandant, the fearless bomber of the Bocche di Cattaro and night-time awakener of the Lion. Iterum rudit Leo. XXVI December MCMXX". "The lion roars again" was the d'Annunzian motto linked to his flight over Cattaro on 4 October 1917, and the phrase does not hide the controversy over the sad conclusion to the Fiume exploit, which the poet saw as a terrible betrayal by the governing authority.

The stained glass window of *Saint Cecilia at the organ*, the patron saint of musicians, here portrayed with the face of the fine pianist, Luisa Baccara, caught in an ecstatic rapture by the music, was designed by Guido Cadorin and made by Pietro Chiesa; the faces of Cadorin and Maroni can be distinguished at the bottom. Forty-one antique polychrome wooden statues of saints stand on the high shelf running along the three walls, while some of the religious paintings, such as the *Head of Christ* by a sixteenth century Venetian school, and the *Good Samaritan*, by a seventeenth century Dutch school, come from Thode's collection. There are also two genuine altars in the room: one is the so-called "pyramid of idols", full of oriental statuettes; the other, a sixteenth century ciborium in gilded wood, is covered with religious symbols, eighteenth century relics and a "bloody relic" as Gabriele called it: the broken steering wheel of the motorboat in which Sir Henry Segrave died in June 1930, during a speed race on the waters of Lake Windermere. Beside it are two Chinese lacquered folding chairs. A display case made of iron and glass contains a processional cross from the first half of the fourteenth century; and to complete the variety of religions on display is the cast of the Praxiteles *Hermes*: d'Annunzio was greatly struck by the original which he saw at Olympia in 1895.

Cucina (Kitchen)

Gabriele was always abstemious with regard to food, and became all the more so over the years. Frequent

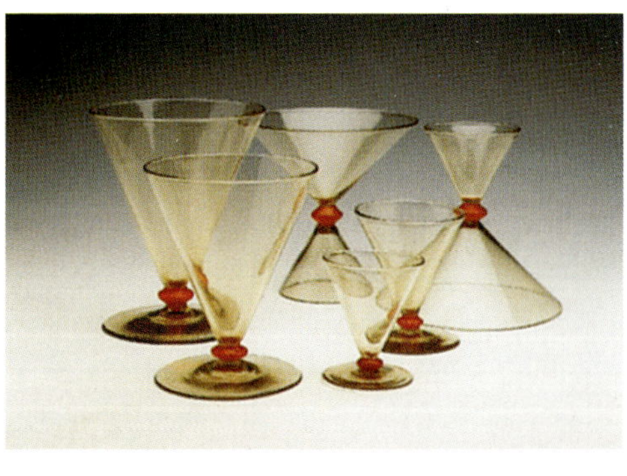

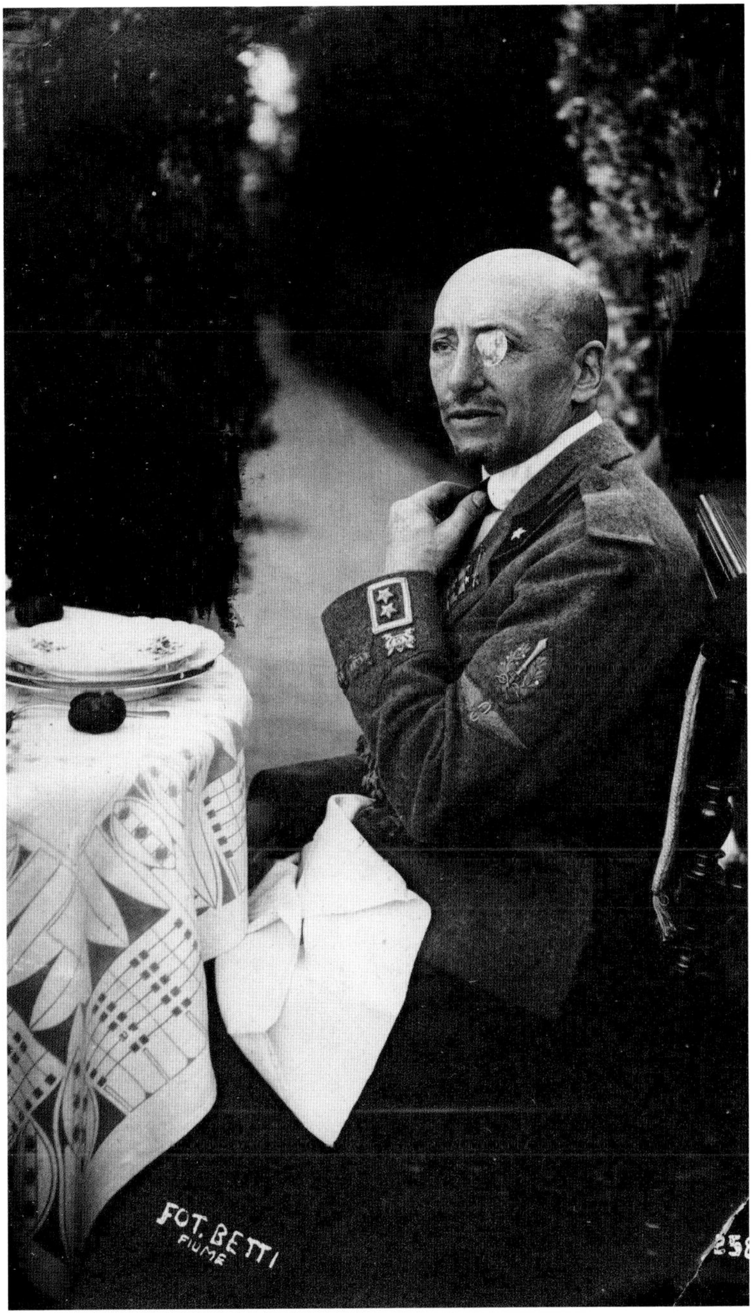

Gabriele d'Annunzio dining in Fiume

stomach problems, a lack of appetite due to his use of drugs and medicines, and lastly his atavistic Abruzzo way of treating problems by fasting ("He would eat nothing for three days, and then three or four eggs all in one go" Ojetti narrates), all caused him to eat little, with the exception of breakfast which he ate with the appetite of an adolescent after an exhausting night of love. He did not drink alcohol (as a "water drinker", he loved and could distinguish "the different tastes and different freshness of drinking water"), and he ate very moderately most of the time, although he greatly appreciated what he called "the culinary arts". His taste for certain "exquisite trifles" is evident in his writings, or from memories of guests delighted by the care and refinement of his table. Dishes such as asparagus, scampi from Grado, veal cutlets, game, Maiella sheep's cheese, water melon, Sicilian oranges, raisins wrapped in vine leaves, mandarins and bergamot oranges from Calabria, "persicata di Brescia" (a dessert with peaches), ice cream, Abruzzo parrozzo (a cake made with chocolate and almonds which he christened and publicized), and chocolates, all served impeccably on the finest tableware (such as the breakfast set designed by Gio Ponti), on silver, crystal or "porcelain matched to the quality of the food" as he himself wrote, aroused in him feelings of immense gratitude towards his cook, Albina Becevello, who had served him faithfully since his wartime experiences, and whom he re-christened "Sister Ghiottizia" or "Sister Intingola". "You will have a marble kitchen and a Throne of fire" the poet wrote to her in one of the many amusing, joking notes he sent her from time to time, requesting something or thanking her for some perfectly cooked dish. And the domain of this sublime craftswoman was indeed a welcoming, practical kitchen.
It is accessed from the "Gamma corridor" (which has a telephone booth at the end, very modern for its time, and a Triton by the German symbolist painter Hans Thoma, which previously belonged to Thode), decorated by a stained glass window showing musical instruments, created by Pietro Chiesa in 1933. The kitchen, painted in a very fresh, "hygienic" blue, consists of three rooms: a central room for preparing the food (with a wood-burning cooking stove, a fireplace, and a hotplate), one for washing up (with a sink), and one for food preservation (with an ice box and electric fridge). Hanging on the walls are copper and ceramic pots and pans and other utensils, some of which are antiques.

Stanza delle Marionette (Room of the Puppets)

A dressing-room and wash-room for guests this room (excluded from the tour itinerary) takes its name from the three eighteenth century Venetian puppets behind the glass cases lining the walls. For d'Annunzio, the politicians and leading figures in political life in the post-First World War years were all "puppets" and "marionettes".

Stanza del Giglio (Room of the Lily)

Going along the Gamma corridor you arrive in the room dedicated to the Lily (the flower of the Annunciation, and thus of the archangel Gabriel), and the title of a series of novels conceived by the poet but not completed, one of which was *The Virgins of the Rock*, published in 1895. Marussig painted the ornamental motifs of the lily and laurel in the niche where the *harmonium* is placed, with its fake aluminium pipes in imitation of an organ (with the inscription inside "minima quoque", "also the details"), and in the two *pensatoi* (thinking areas) which evoke the isolation necessary for study and literature. The bookshelves hold about three thousand books, mainly of Italian history and of literature.

Oratorio Dalmata (Dalmatian Oratory)

The room immediately next to it is the "Oratorio dalmata" – access to which could be closed off by a heavy curtain – named after the *Lion of Dalmatia* that stands on top of a column. This was the waiting room for guests, who were then led into two rooms that were originally dining rooms, now the *Stanza delle Reliquie* and the *Stanza del Mappamondo*. The fireplace in Verona broccatello marble, designed by Maroni, is inscribed with the phrase from St Francis's *Canticle of the Creatures*: "Praise be to you, my Lord, through Brother Fire, through whom you brighten the night; he is beautiful and cheerful, and powerful and strong."
The quiet atmosphere invites meditation, enhanced by the books of prayer and spiritual exercise, missals, candelabras, censers, aspergillums, thuribles, eighteenth century reliquary busts, a casket in enamelled copper by Giuseppe Guidi in imitation of the medieval reliquaries of Limoges, and sacred images: a *Madonna with Child*, a *Christ crowned with thorns*, a seventeenth century *Head of Saint Sebastian*, a *Job Covered with Boils* from the first half of the seventeenth century by the Jusepe de Ribera

Room of the Lily

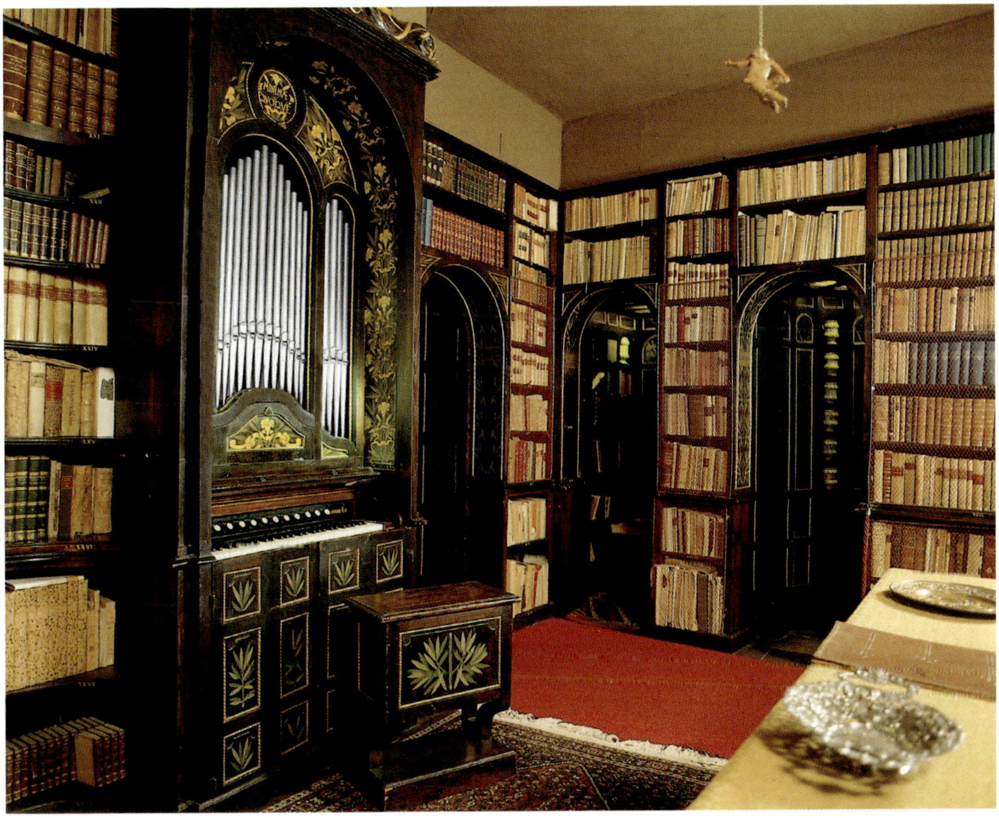

workshop, and a painting of *Faith* (in the space below). Among some of the other "profane" objects is a donkey yoke of Abruzzo craftsmanship, previously in the Capponcina, and, hanging from the ceiling, the wooden propeller from the seaplane with which Francesco de Pinedo completed his feat in 1925 (a flight of 55,000 kilometres from Sesto Calende to Japan, Australia and back to Rome), which was a gift to the poet from the aviator himself.

On the western wall there is a rose-coloured marble drinking fountain with a votive lamp which was always lit, in memory of the beloved mother, Luisa; the lamp is inscribed with another phrase from St Francis: "Praise be to you, my lord, for Sister Water, who is very useful and humble, and precious and pure."

In his atmosphere saturated with symbols and religious references, an inscription on the door leading to the entrance vestibule reads: "Ego sum Gabriel qui asto ante deos / alitis de fratribus unus oculeos / Postverta alumnus / arcani divini minister / humanae dementiae sequester / volucer demissus ab alto / princeps et praeco" ("I am Gabriele, and I present myself before the gods / of all the noble brothers the most far-seeing / a pupil of Postverta / high priest of the arcane and the divine / interpreter of human insanity / the flying one fallen from on high / prince and prophet"). This long inscription is dense with references: Gabriele, archangel and therefore "brother" of the angels, who was said to be "the seeing eye" after the wartime accident in 1916 that deprived him of the sight of his right eye, Vate (*Bard*) (according to Roman mythology, the goddess Postverta could foresee the future) recalls here the so-called "flight of the Archangel".

Dalmatian Oratory

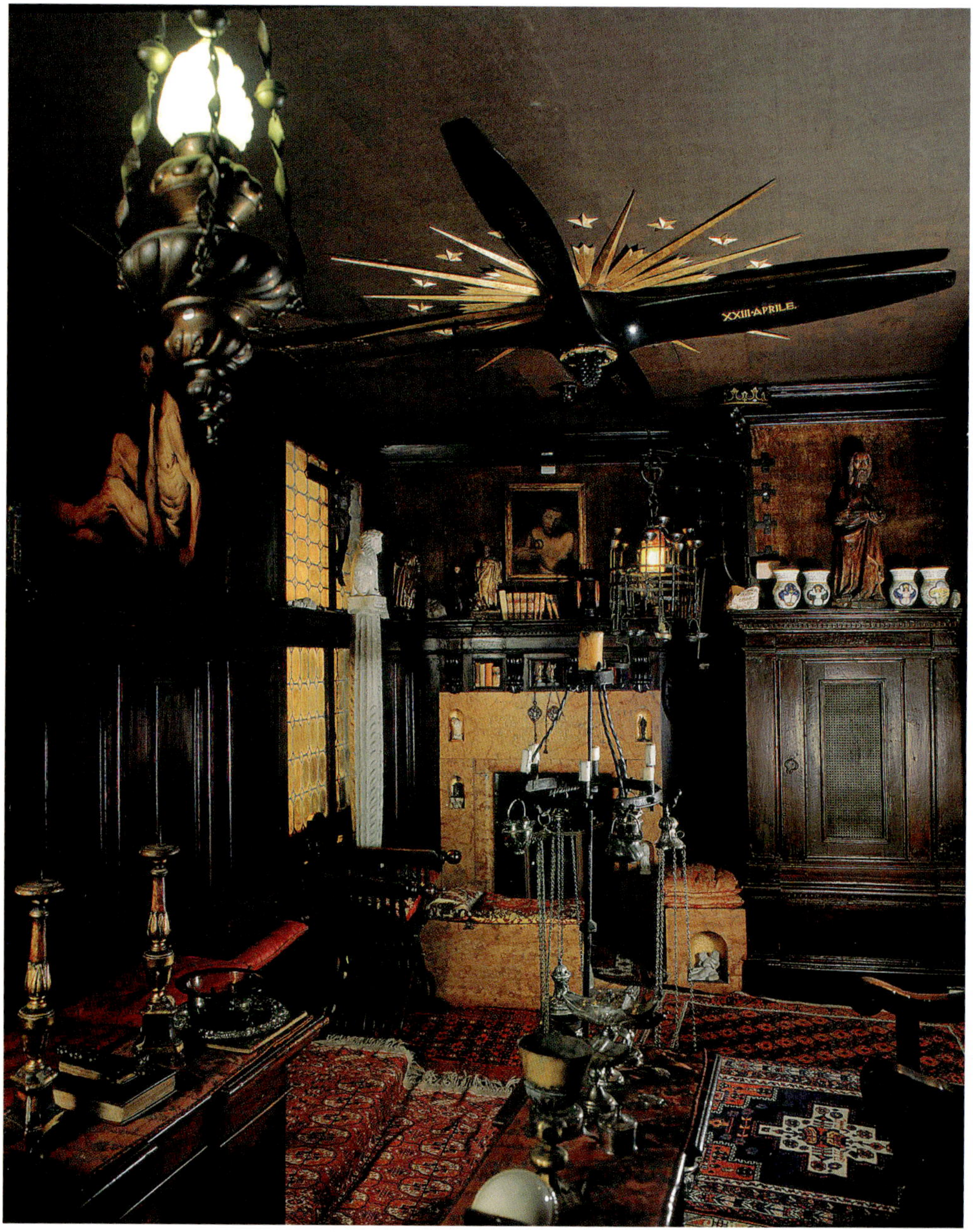

Desk of the Mutilated One

The motto of the mutilated hand at the entrance to the Desk of the Mutilated One

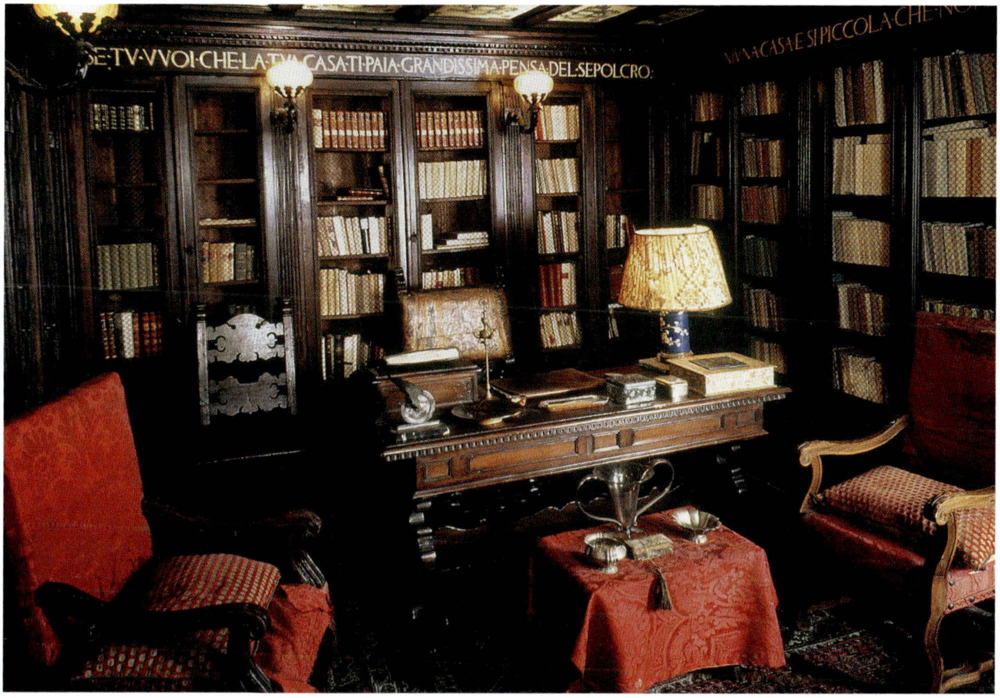

Scrittoio del Monco (Desk of the Mutilated One)

Immersed in the quiet, almost mystical atmosphere of the Oratorio dalmata, the guest is invited to pass through a wooden door, and then to go up a narrow passageway lined with books, and with small sculptures and objects in niches in the wall. Various mottos are displayed on the walls, including "Pax et Bonum / Bonum et Pax" (Peace and Goodwill / Goodwill and Peace), "Ave / Cave / Pave" ("Welcome / Be careful / Be afraid"), and at the bottom, "Aliquid amplius invenies / in silvis quam in libris" ("You will find more in woods than in books").

Beyond the landing, which has two early eighteenth century wooden sculptures standing in niches, you come to a door on the right, which has, carved into the architrave, a severed, flayed hand, red with blood, with the motto "Recisa quiescit" ("It rests when it is severed"). It is the entrance to the Scrittoio del monco, the study d'Annunzio used for his correspondence, which was so burdensome (letters, requests, various communications, all of which are catalogued and stored in the Vittoriale archives) that in 1926 d'Annunzio decided to obtain a tape recorder so he could dictate his answers without tiring himself out writing them. On the door is a hand, with the Spanish motto picked out in nails: "Con l'altra" and, on the inside of the door, the same hand with "Buena fe no es mudable" ("good faith is not changeable"). On the coffered

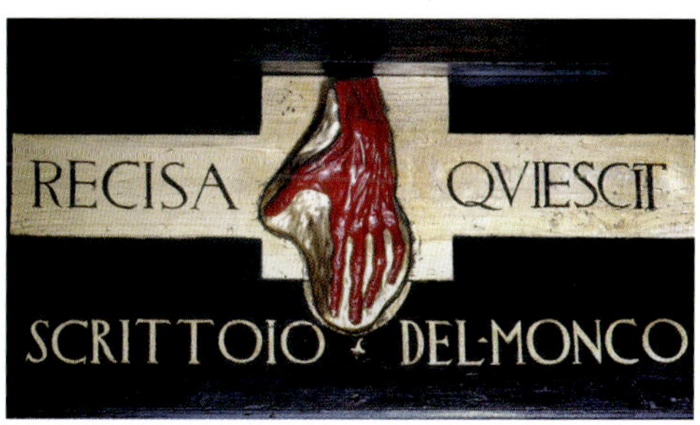

ceiling, painted by Marussig, there is the same hand in an iron glove with the inscriptions "Tuerto y derecho" and "Todo es nada" ("Crooked and straight" and "All is nothing").
It is a simple room, with walls covered in bookshelves previously at the Capponcina (Italian and French literature) rescued from the auction in 1911. Along the upper ledges are four phrases taken from Leonardo da Vinci's writings: "Acciocché tu più cose possa, più ne sostieni"; "No house is so small that it is not made large by a great inhabitant"; "If you want your house to seem very big, think of the tomb"; "Those who have no burial place are covered by the sky". The longer walls have imitations of the emblems from the study of Isabella d'Este in the Palazzo Ducale in Mantova, a frequent source of inspiration for d'Annunzio's mottos: "Nec Spe nec Metu" ("neither hope nor fear"), XXVII, musical rests on the stave and the Greek letters ωα alternating with αω the beginning and the end. Among the objects is a splendid *Dragonfly Vase* in rose-coloured blown glass by Vittorio Zecchin, designed for the Muranese glass company Venini in 1923.
A door made in the early 1930s allows direct access to the Torre degli Archivi via the loggia.

Officina (Workshop)
This was the inevitable name for d'Annunzio's study, since he loved to call himself a "wordsmith" and, from his early youth, worked tenaciously, consulting dictionaries, and grammar books to refine his use of the language, succeeding in achieving mastery of it in the rich-

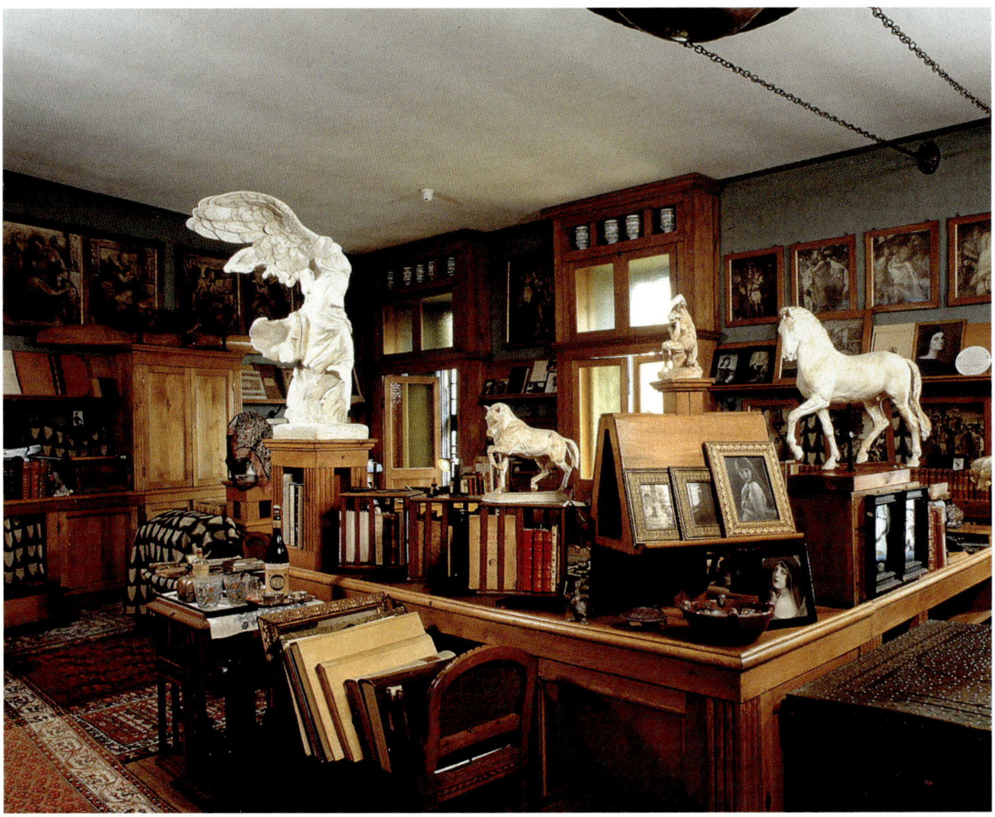

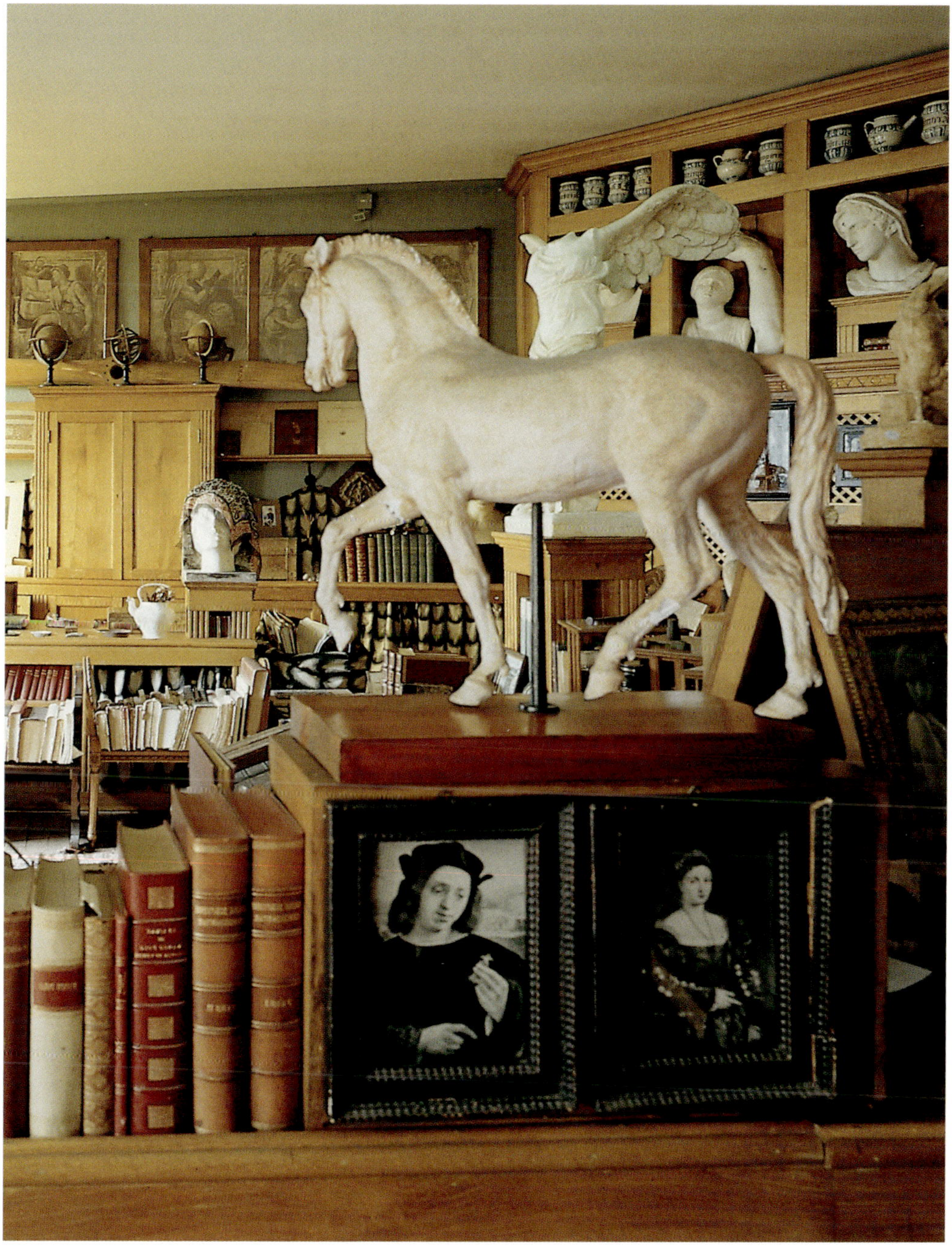

ness of his use of adjectives, nouns and verbs, that were always precise, refined and accurate.
This room, completed in 1926, is furnished with functional furniture in light-coloured oak and is accessed by steps, which makes people have to bow their heads in a sign of humility. The motto inscribed on the architrave is taken from Virgil (*Aeneid*, VI, 129), "Hoc opus, hic labor est" ("This is the labour, this is the toil"), and at the centre there is a plaster cast of a French Gothic bas-relief depicting *Saint Matthew Writing the Gospel Inspired by the Angel*, an evident allusion to the chosen, divine work of the poet. A second door with spy-holes emphasizes the room's secret nature and the difficulty of access, and indeed very few people were permitted to enter. Inside, there is abundant light from the three large French windows, reflected on the white ceiling and pale green walls, making it an exceptional environment compared to the semi-darkness dominating nearly all the other rooms in the house.
On the walls, above the black and white "vair" fabric made by the Lisio company from Florence, are the Alinari photographs of works by Mantegna (the *Triumphs*), Botticelli and Michelangelo (the *Sybils* from the Sistine Chapel, the Medici tombs), as well as plaster casts of the Metopes, the internal frieze from the Parthenon and the *Nike of Samothrace*, "without their glaring whiteness and expertly suffused with an uneven ivory patina", made from coffee by d'Annunzio himself, "the master of patinators", as we read in his *Libro segreto*; this mixture of ancient and Renaissance art reflects his constant reference to the sublime models of the art of the past.
Dictionaries, catalogues, leather folders for filing pages of manuscript are arranged on the desks, shelves, and book rests, as evidence of the poet's continual, practical work. The shelves and bookcases at an angle to the floor were made by the carpenter Isaia Scarpetta from a design by Maroni and indications from d'Annunzio, modelled on Renaissance studies and the shelves painted by Carpaccio in his *Vision of Saint Augustine*. Above the bookcases are engraved and gilded wooden scrolls with the inscriptions: "Acciocché tu cose più possa più ne sostieni"; "L'ouvrier se cognoist à l'ouvrage"; "Lego piegandomi" "Laissez moi penser à mon ayse". To provide inspiration for Gabriele in his creativity is the "veiled witness", *Eleonora Duse*, in a plaster cast of the sculpture portrait of her by Arrigo Minerbi (the marble original is still preserved at the Vittoriale), which d'Annunzio kept covered with a silk cloth.

Corridoio del Labirinto (Labyrinth Corridor)

About two thousand volumes of French literature are collected here, bound in leather with the emblem of the labyrinth used for the cover of the "Forse che sì, forse che no" ("Maybe yes, maybe no") novel published in Milan in 1910. The title was inspired by an ancient Tuscan proverb which became the chorus of a popular song common in the fifteenth century in the duchy of Mantova. Isabella d'Este had it written down and inscribed on the passages of a maze, together with other mottos she liked, in the rooms of her apartments in Corte Vecchia, in the Palazzo Ducale. D'Annunzio had seen them and had the motto and labyrinth later copied into the decorations at the Vittoriale. Other mottos in the wooden scrolls above the shelves, refer to work and to the creative passion that uplifts man: "Lege lege et relege"; "Labora ora et invenies"; "E per nodo e per forza"; "Doppio ardor mi consuma"; "Ardisco non ordisco"; "Le temps verra"; "Ardendo m'inalzo".

Stanza della Cheli (Room of the Cheli)

This room, started in 1926 and completed in 1929, was the dining room and it links the Prioria with Schifamondo. Also called the *Cenacolo dell'angelo* (the angel's dining room) (Gabriele called himself "the angel of abstinence" and liked to project an image of himself as someone who never made himself vulgar by eating too much), the name comes from the tortoise given to d'Annunzio by the Marchesa Luisa Casati, which died of indigestion after eating too many roots in the splendid *Prioria* garden.
D'Annunzio entrusted Renato Brozzi, the fine chiseller and "animal sculptor of the Vittoriale", with the task of modelling a bronze sculpture from the shell of the Cheli (*khélis* is the Greek for tortoise), as a perpetual admonition to temperance – also alluded to in the *Fat Buddha* and *Thin Buddha* on the Chinese table. The bronze scroll is engraved with the words "Intra me maneo" ("I remain inside myself"), an allusion to

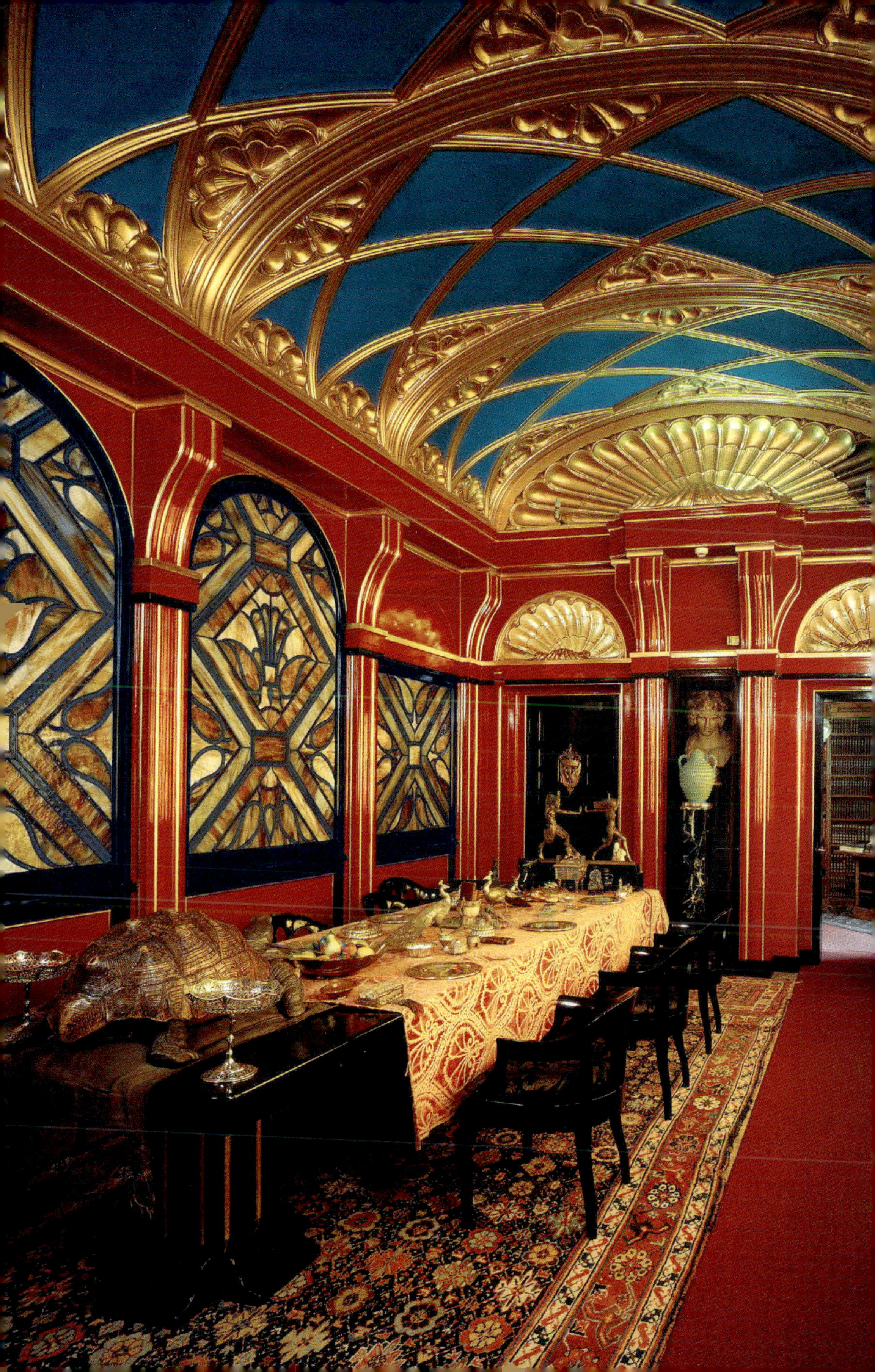

Pierre Le Faguays,
Satyr chasing a nymph

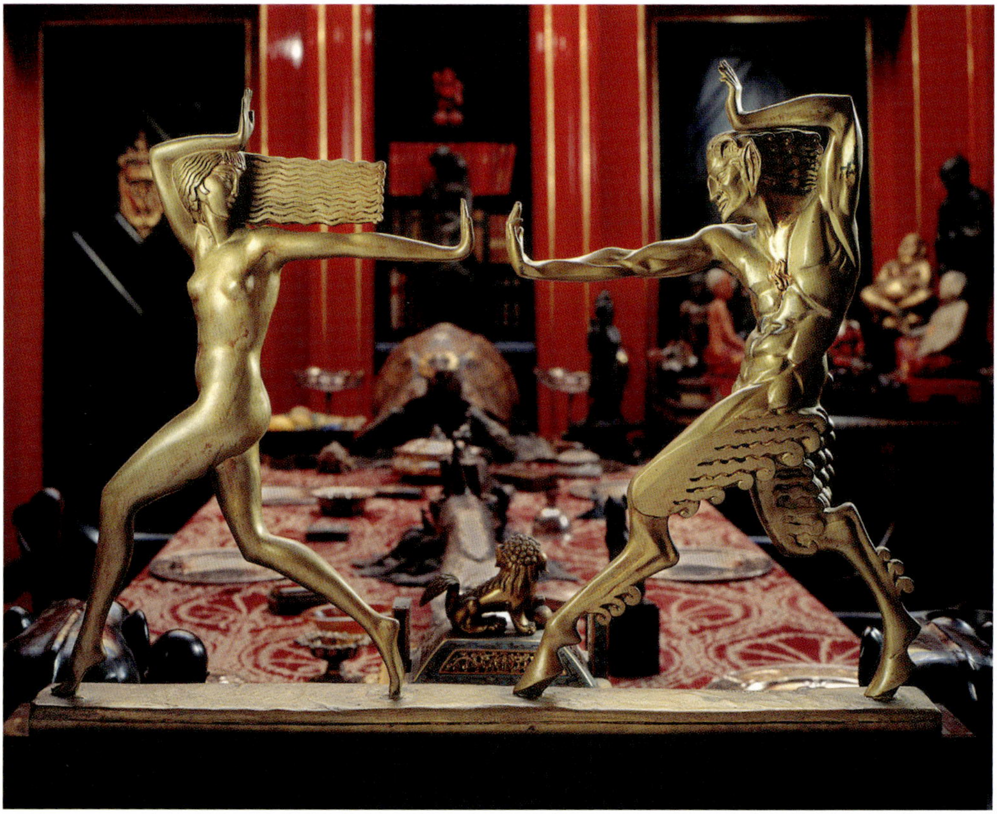

the poet's state of voluntary reclusion inside his splendid residence.
"I'm not planning a monastic refectory," d'Annunzio wrote to Maroni as the room was being planned, and when the work was completed he could claim: "It is the only room in the Vittoriale that is not sad." In fact, the colours of the walls and ceiling, the large golden shells in the blue lozenges on the ceiling and the panel above the door, the brilliant red, gold and black lacquer, and the golden light filtering in through the alabaster windows of Pietro Chiesa all contribute to the warm, welcoming atmosphere of the room. D'Annunzio, who was the perfect host but hardly ever dined in the company of his guests, wanted his table to be perpetually and sumptuously laid; and so, in addition to the *Cheli*, there are two silver peacocks and some smaller ones, enamelled and encrusted with precious stones, the "Franciscan dishes" (embossed silver under-dishes) by Brozzi, and the bronze group of a *Satyr chasing a nymph* created by the French artist Pierre Le Faguays in 1925. In a beautifully placed niche, behind a silver lamé mesh to conceal such disturbing beauty, is the bust of *Antinous* as Dionysius, a copy of the original Roman work reproducing the features of emperor Hadrian's beautiful young Greek lover, who died mysteriously in the waters of the river Nile and was mourned by the emperor who decided to make him divine. In front of this is a French ceramic vase from the 1920s.
On the opposite walls there is a bronze monkey by Giacinto Bardetti.

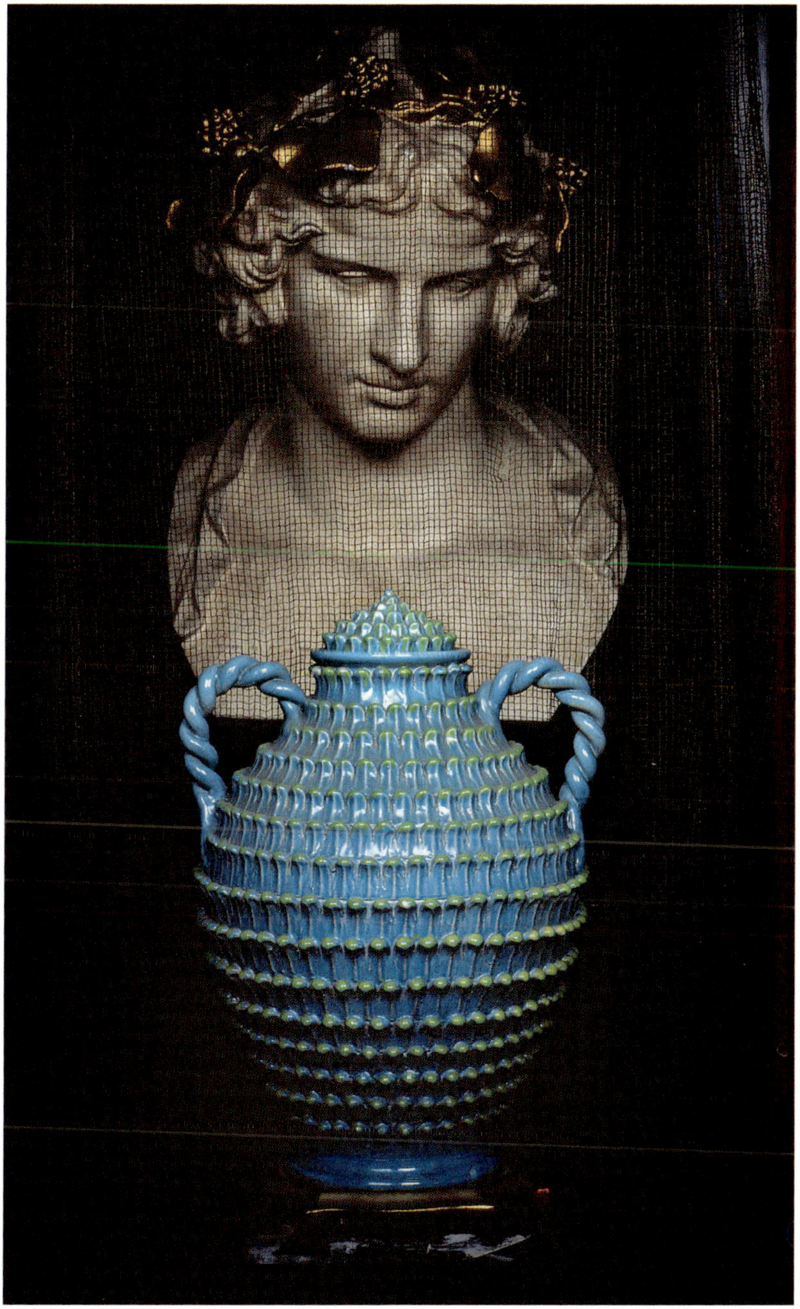

Plaster cast
of the *Antinoo*

Francesco Nonni,
Pierrot

Female Guests'
Bathroom

Appartamenti delle Ospiti
(Female Guests' Apartments)

On the first floor, screened off by a wooden lattice door opening onto the landing of the Officina, are the "enclosed" apartments (excluded from the tour itinerary), where the two women who managed the house during d'Annunzio's retreat of almost twenty years at the Vittoriale, lived in rather difficult co-habitation: the poet's companion, Luisa Baccara, constantly betrayed, very jealous yet incapable of leaving him and the French housekeeper Aélis Mazoyer. But d'Annunzio's numerous female guests also stayed here, in a small guestroom: friends, lovers for a few months or a year – like some of the enamoured noblewomen whose letters have been preserved – or occasional visitors and sometimes paying guests. The demanding and imaginative host and insatiable lover provided this place for them to wash, perfume and dress themselves in the light, fine underwear and fabrics (still preserved in the cupboards) that he himself had designed – "Gabriel Nuncius Vestiarius" – or ordered from the atelier of the famous Milanese tailor Biki. All of them were subject to a seductive attention involving all five senses: Gabriele conquered and amazed his numerous women through music, the exquisitely laid table, rustling fabrics, perfumes, and the beauty of art. So it is not surprising to find, skimming through his private correspondence preserved in the Vittoriale archives, the sincere outpourings of young, beautiful, high-ranking women, many of them married, who had fallen head over heels in love with the aging poet whose appearance, in the last few years, definitely showed the marks of time.

The rooms in this private area of the villa, which, like a true harem, was never open to public view, were furnished with a bourgeois simplicity: pale colours, dolls, nineteenth century furniture, toiletries, and prints and copies of eighteenth century paintings, although there was the occasional more modern touch, such as the typically twentieth century style cornucopia chandelier by Napoleone Martinuzzi, in Aélis's room. The bathrooms are more original, such as the guest bathroom which is entirely in dark purple, with a niche display-

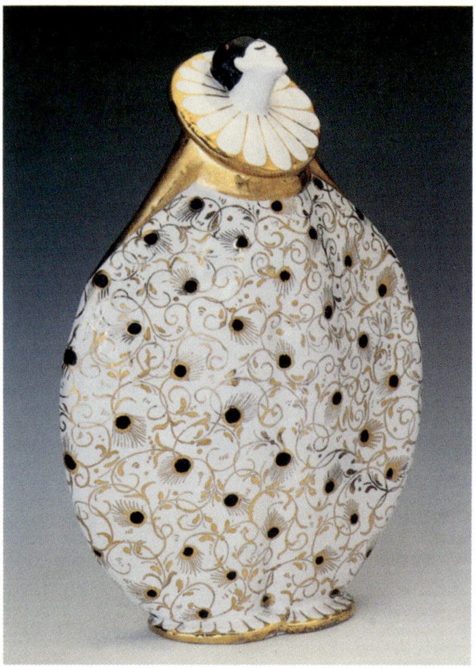

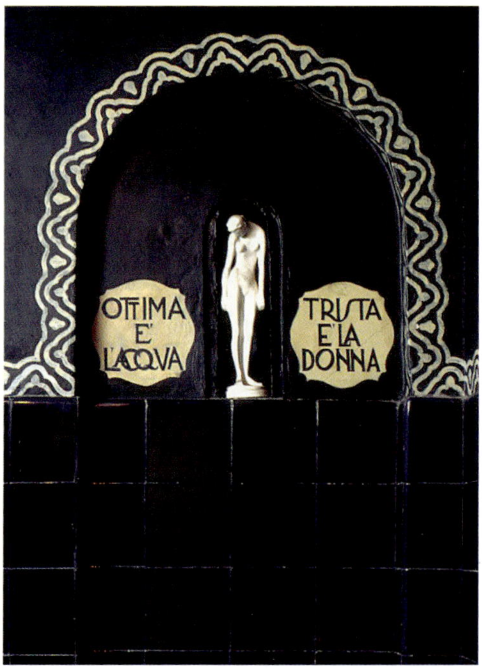

ing the words "Water is the best of all – Sad is the woman". The slender nude figure of a woman in white majolica is by Milanese craftsman Enrico Mazzolani, who also made the large female figure, the *Song of the Sun*, in polychrome majolica. The porcelain pieces by Rosenthal, the *Prince* and the *Princess*, designed by the German Gerhard Schliepstein in 1925, and the *Pierrot* by Faenza craftsman Francesco Nonni, are also very fine.

Giardino della Prioria (Prioria's Garden)

"The living flower adds to the fineness of the work of art; and the work of art adds to the enchantment of the living flower" d'Annunzio wrote in the *Taccuini*.
And indeed, flowers, flowers and more flowers emerge from d'Annunzio's writings and habits. Roses act as a mirror to full female beauty in the pages of *Piacere*: "She entered, with a large swathe of roses in her pinafore and in her arms – pink, white, yellow, crimson, and dark red. Some large and pale [...]; others with dense petals [...]; some seemed like handfuls of scented snow [...]; others were flesh, real flesh, voluptuous as the most voluptuous forms of a woman's body [...]." Or the hyacinths, violets, and orange blossom with their "innocent, sharp, infantile" perfumes, bringing an emotional, olfactory pang in the pages of the *Notturno*, when, during his blind, painful convalescence in bed, Gabriele momentarily recovered the sweetness of the senses through a bunch of flowers, damp with rain. Then there were the flowers given to and by Luisa Baccara in every stage of their relationship, tuberous flowers and branches of oleander with the scent of "vanilla". Flowers on the pennants of the Fiumi legionnaires ("I have tied almond and peach blossom to the flagpoles" he wrote to Luisa Baccara in March 1920). Or again, "the first lilac flower, white: a small thick cluster of dense, dense flowers on a bare stem;" or the first camellia from his garden, which he records in a note one February, without giving the year: he describes it as "small, waxy, with dense, fleshy petals, and waxy flesh, a fresh, living thing" that "harmonizes better than any other flower with fine works of art."
D'Annunzio, who had a very refined sense of smell, was one of the few poets able through his poetry to suggest every smell and every colour, and who loved, knew and recognised the nuances and scents of herbs, plants, and flowers which he wrote about in his books, and with which he surrounded himself, arranging them harmoniously in vases of very fine Murano glass until, as an old man, disturbed by their inevitable disintegration, he wanted only glass flowers around him.
To serve this, one of his many needs, superfluous yet necessary, during his long residence in the Vittoriale, was the superb garden of cypresses, olive trees, palm trees, rose gardens, and magnolias, sloping down towards the lake and cared for by trusted staff. D'Annunzio's gardens could not fail to be beautiful, the inevitable development of that continual, striking, artistic and theatrical staging that is the Vittoriale. The *garden* is now accessible from the entrance to the right of the *Prioria*, but d'Annunzio had access to it through a flight of steps in the house, along the *Corridoio della Via Crucis* and across the *Cortile degli Schiavoni*, with its three ancient Venetian wells, next to the *Portico del parente*.
The *Portico* is the area before the gardens which was used in summer, suitably arrayed with rugs and furniture, as a pleasant open air area. It is dedicated to Michelangelo, the "parente" or "relative", the sublime artist whom the poet felt was the ideal ancestor, and to whom he devoted pages, reflections and scattered notes over the years. To make this area all the more precious and full of memories there are fragments, inscriptions, coats of arms, terracotta heads, sculptures in different materials, and a late fifteenth century monastic lavabo. Among the other works are a plaster cast of the *Torso del Belvedere* (the same copy was in the apartment in Palazzo Borghese which he rented during his stay in Rome as a young man), and the bust of *Michelangelo* by Napoleone Martinuzzi. The frescos are by Guido Marussig, the Trieste painter, stage designer, and illustrator who had sensitively carried out many of d'Annunzio's projects since 1922 (designs for stained glass and decorative panels). From the portico you continue through a door with the inscription "Rosam cape, spinam cave" ("pick the rose, be careful of its thorns") engraved on the architrave, beneath a copy of the *Landolina Venus*. Just beyond the door, in confirmation of d'Annunzio's increasing "Franciscan" tendencies, there is a bronze statue of *Saint Francis*, by the Rome sculptor Giacinto Bardetti, together with a high relief depicting the *Lion of Sebenico*, and various rocks (to be arranged "with rhythm" Gabriele wrote to Maroni), transported here from the most important

Gardens

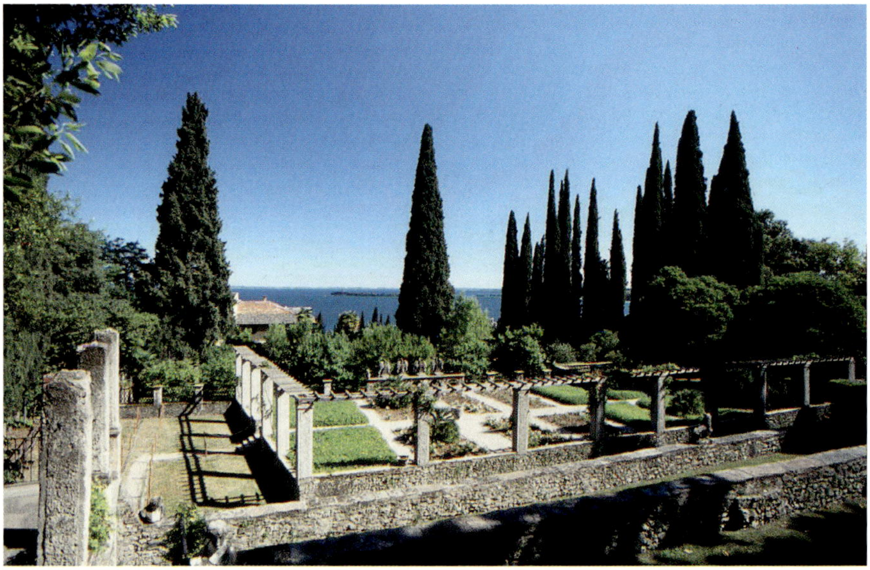

Napoleone Martinuzzi,
Canefora

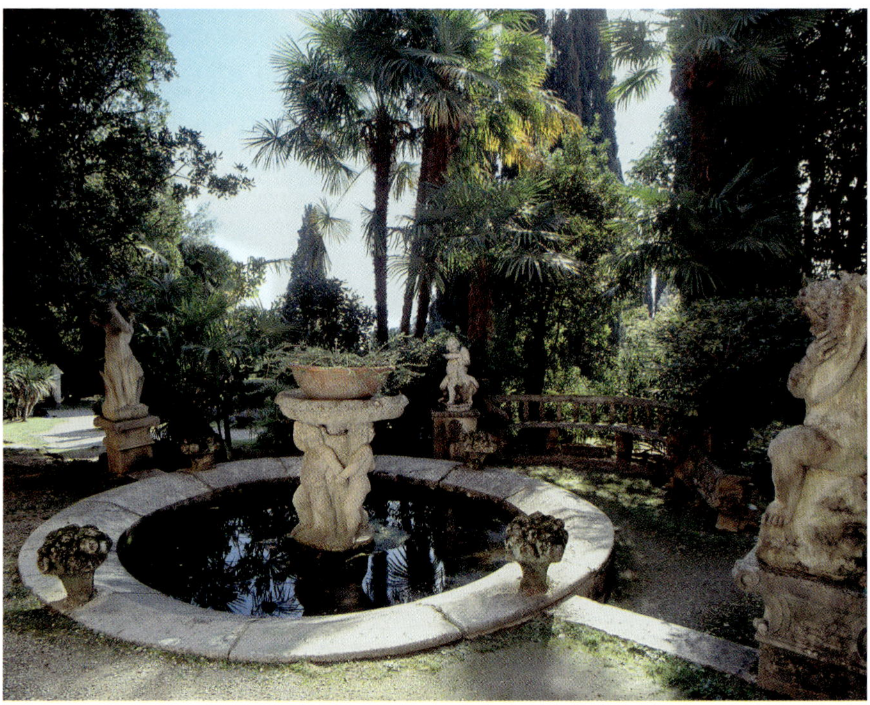

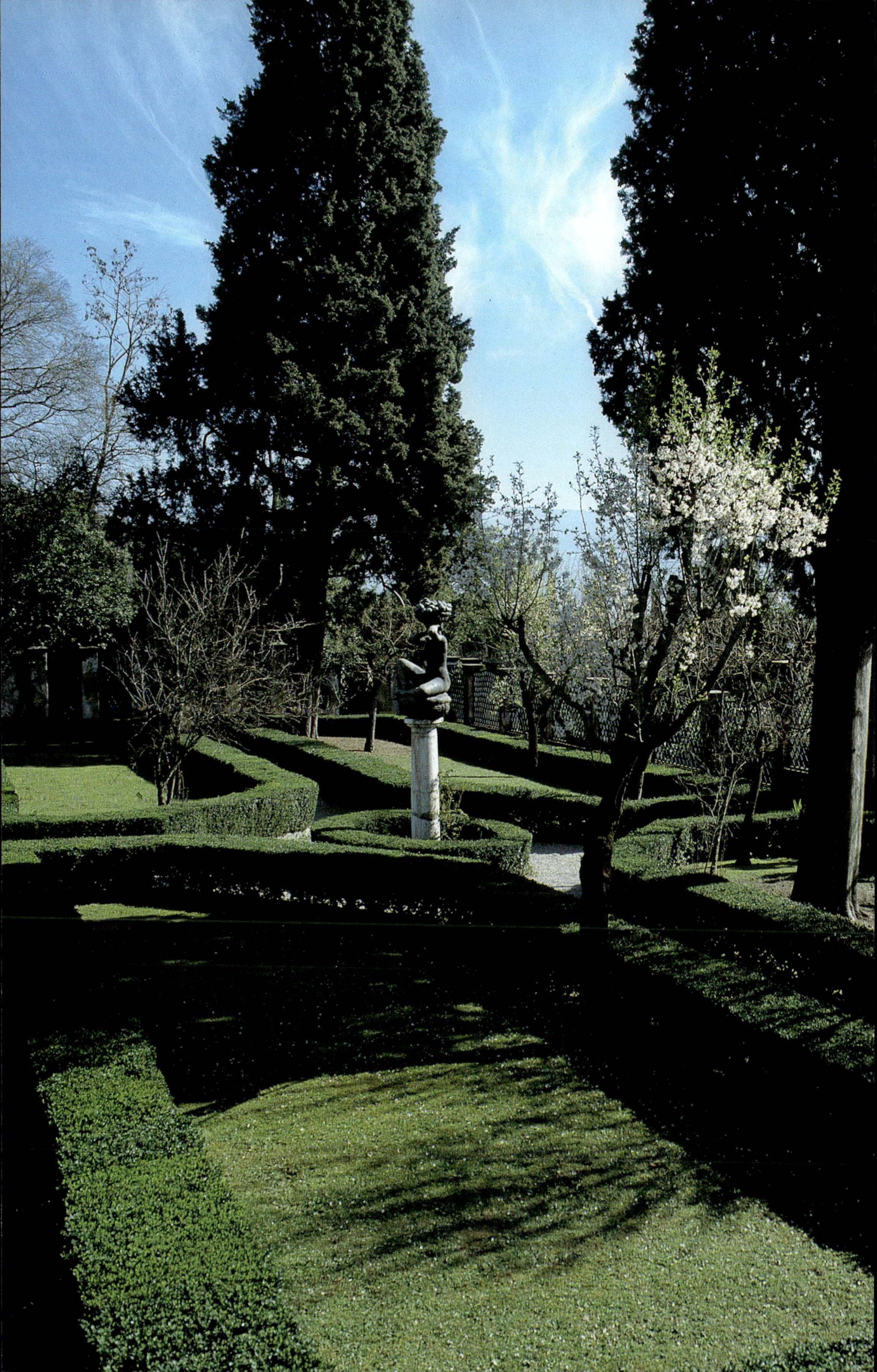

Perimeter wall
of the orchard

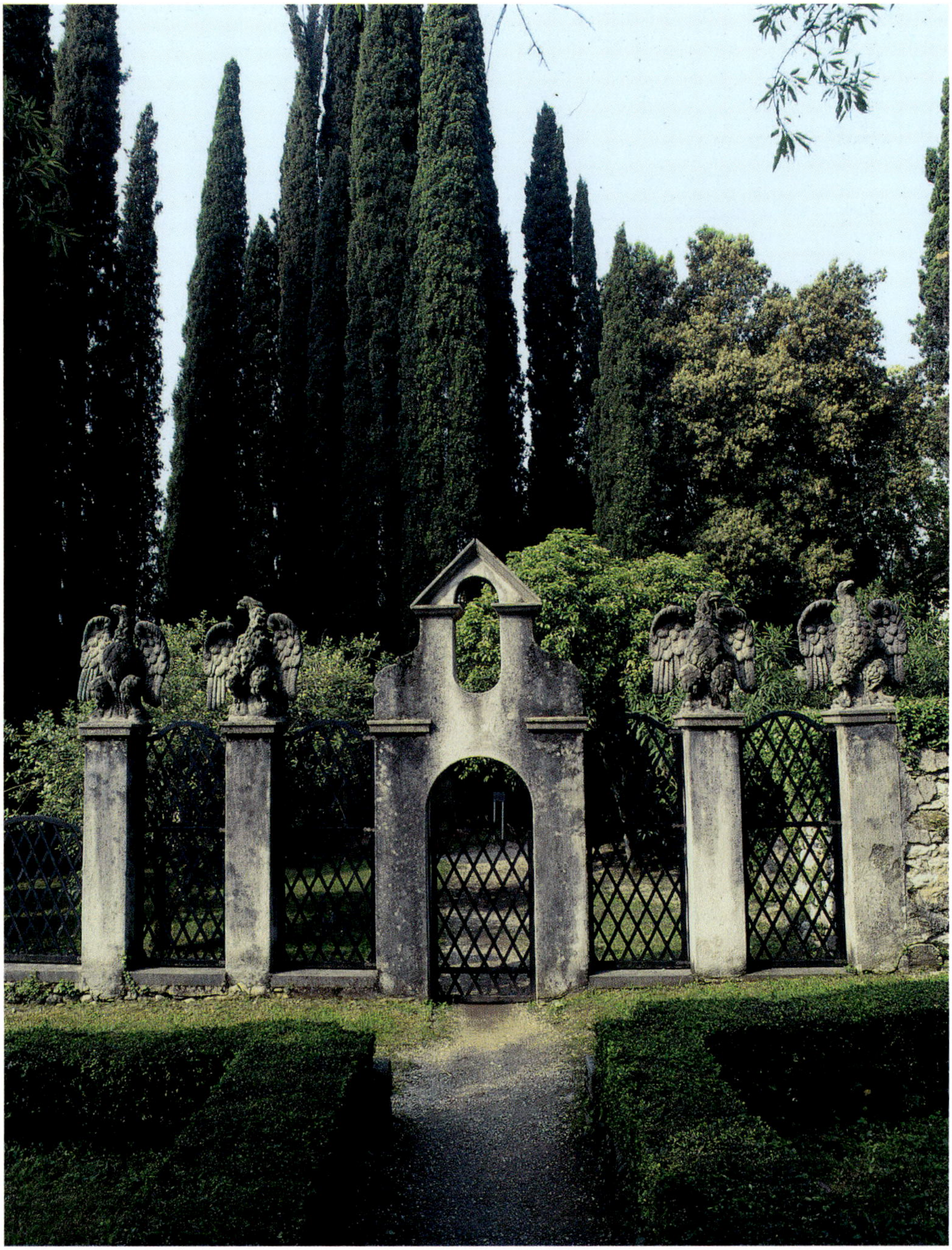

Portico
del Parente
in a period
arrangement

Gabriele
d'Annunzio
in Fiume

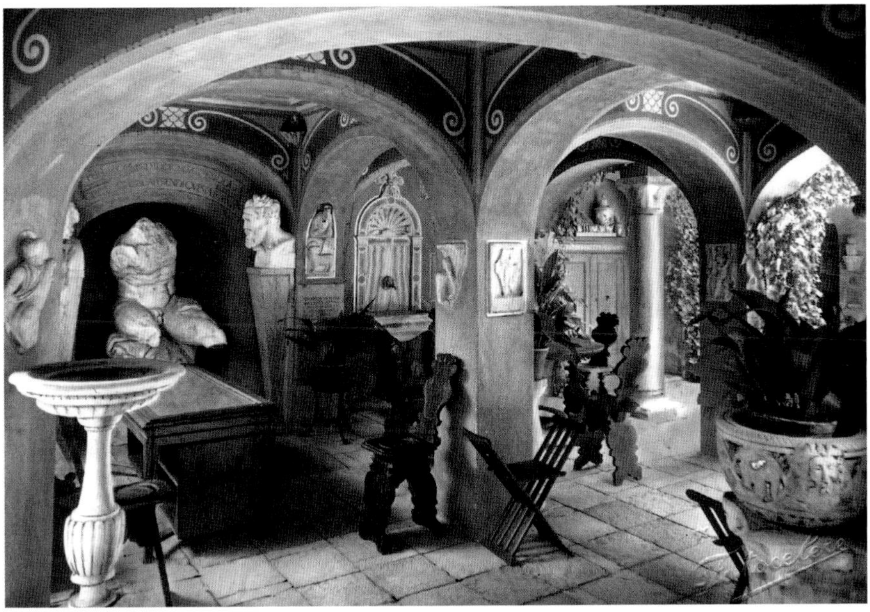

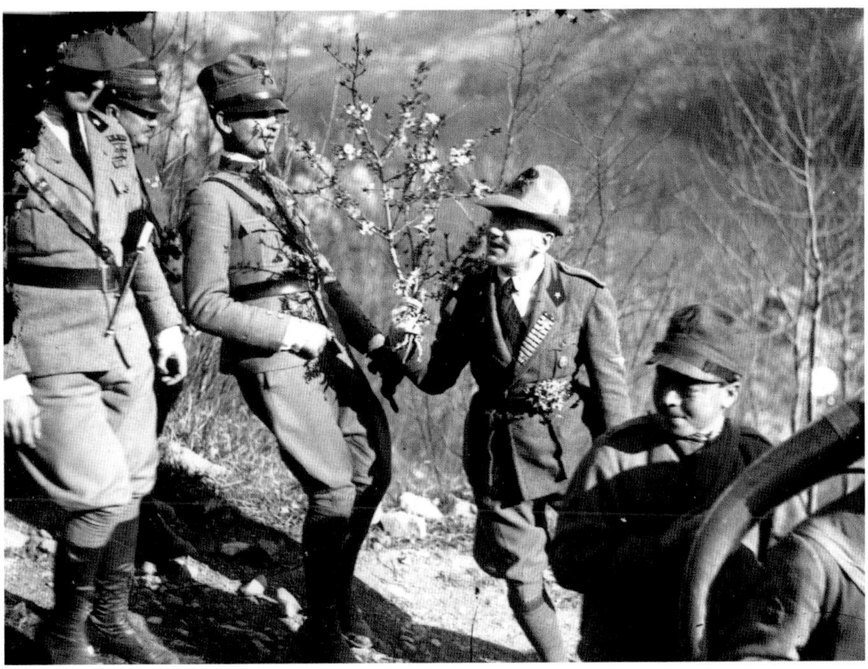

Arengo

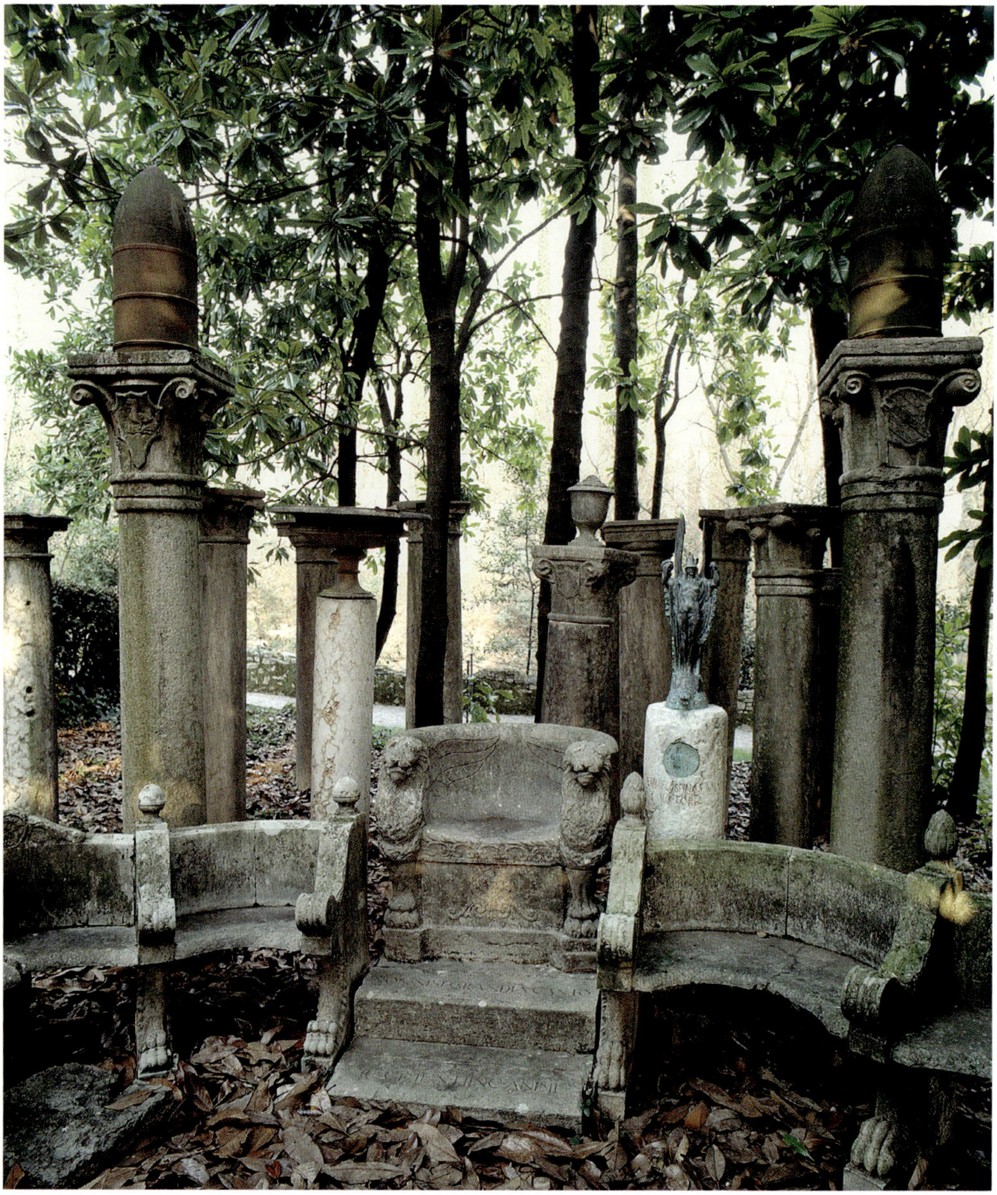

Gabriele d'Annunzio
in the Arengo

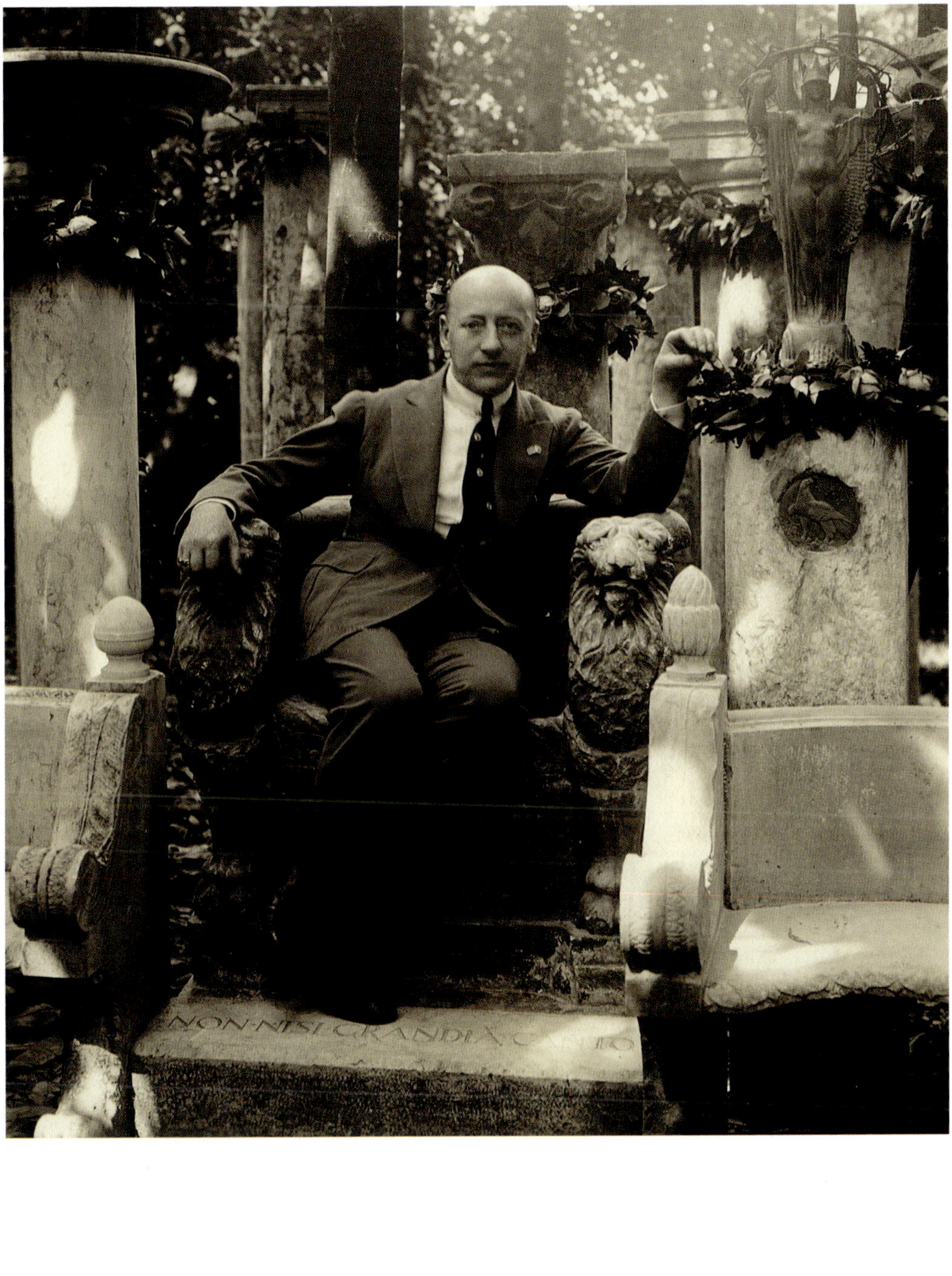

battlegrounds of the First World War, in perpetual memory of that tragedy and as an admonition to humility and human understanding.
To the right there is a stone fountain and to the left, in a magnolia grove, the *Arengo*. For special commemorative occasions, d'Annunzio would meet here with Fiumi legionnaires. Engraved on the steps of his high stone seat – flanked by other, more simple seats for his comrades-in-arms, the so-called "seats of the reprobates" – and decorated with two Venice lions, are the words: "Non nisi guardia canto" ("I will not sing except of great events"and on the first step "Regimen hinc animi" ["Here starts the soul's regime"], phrase used as epigraph of the *Libro segreto*). Seventeen columns, some topped with iron battle shells donated by General Armando Diaz, commemorate the victories of the war; the column dedicated to Caporetto is dark, and surmounted by an urn with earth from the Karst. At the centre is the *Colonna del Giuramento* (*Column of the Oath*), with an iron lectern and a Byzantine capital; the motto reads: "Undique fidus, undique firmus" ("Everywhere faithful, everywhere steadfast").
The bronze of *Victory crowned with thorns*, with the words "Et haec spinas amat Victoria", was commissioned from the Venetian sculptor and master glass craftsman Napoleone Martinuzzi, "Fra Napé", in 1922. Beyond this striking place with its intense memories, the view extends down over terraces of citrus fruit trees, dotted with late eighteenth century statues. From the other side, the view is marked by the Pilum of the Regency of Carnaro and by the St Mark Columns, on which the Gonfalon of St. Mark was hoisted, a gift from the war veterans and the Marine Pact (the name given to the Pact of the "Federation of Italian Sea Workers" established by d'Annunzio in 1923). Further to the side is the tomb of Renata, d'Annunzio's much loved daughter by Maria Gravina, nicknamed the "little mermaid", to whom he devoted some very moving pages in the *Notturno*.
The *orchard* is separated from the garden by a *belvedere*: on the outer wall are stone eagles standing on pillars similar to those of the "hundred fountains" in the Villa d'Este at Tivoli, one of the places that the poet loved to visit during the youthful period he spent in Rome (he called them "alerioni" [little eagles] in *Il Piacere*, describing them in the garden of the imaginary Villa Schifanoja). The *Canefora* (a soft, squatting female figure, carrying a basket full of fruit on her head), cast in bronze by Napoleone Martinuzzi, dates from 1927 and is placed on another pillar among pomegranate trees, the ancient symbol of fertility and plenty.

Schifamondo

Returning to the *Piazzetta Dalmata*, the entrance to Schifamondo is on the left. In the desire to live in an building that was architecturally more modern and in line with the stylistic trends of the early Thirties, d'Annunzio had a new wing built in place of the old farmhouse, next to the Prioria. "I have an almost tragic need to live in a new house," he wrote to Maroni in 1929. In actual fact, d'Annunzio never moved into this "new house", whose novelty lay in the style dominating the rooms and furnishings with a rigorous rationalist-style simplicity.
Following its restoration in 2000, Schifamondo is now the site of the War Museum. Objects, clothing and flags provide reminders of the undertakings – courageous, but perhaps to a greater extent fantastical – with which d'Annunzio astounded public opinion in Europe during the First World War.

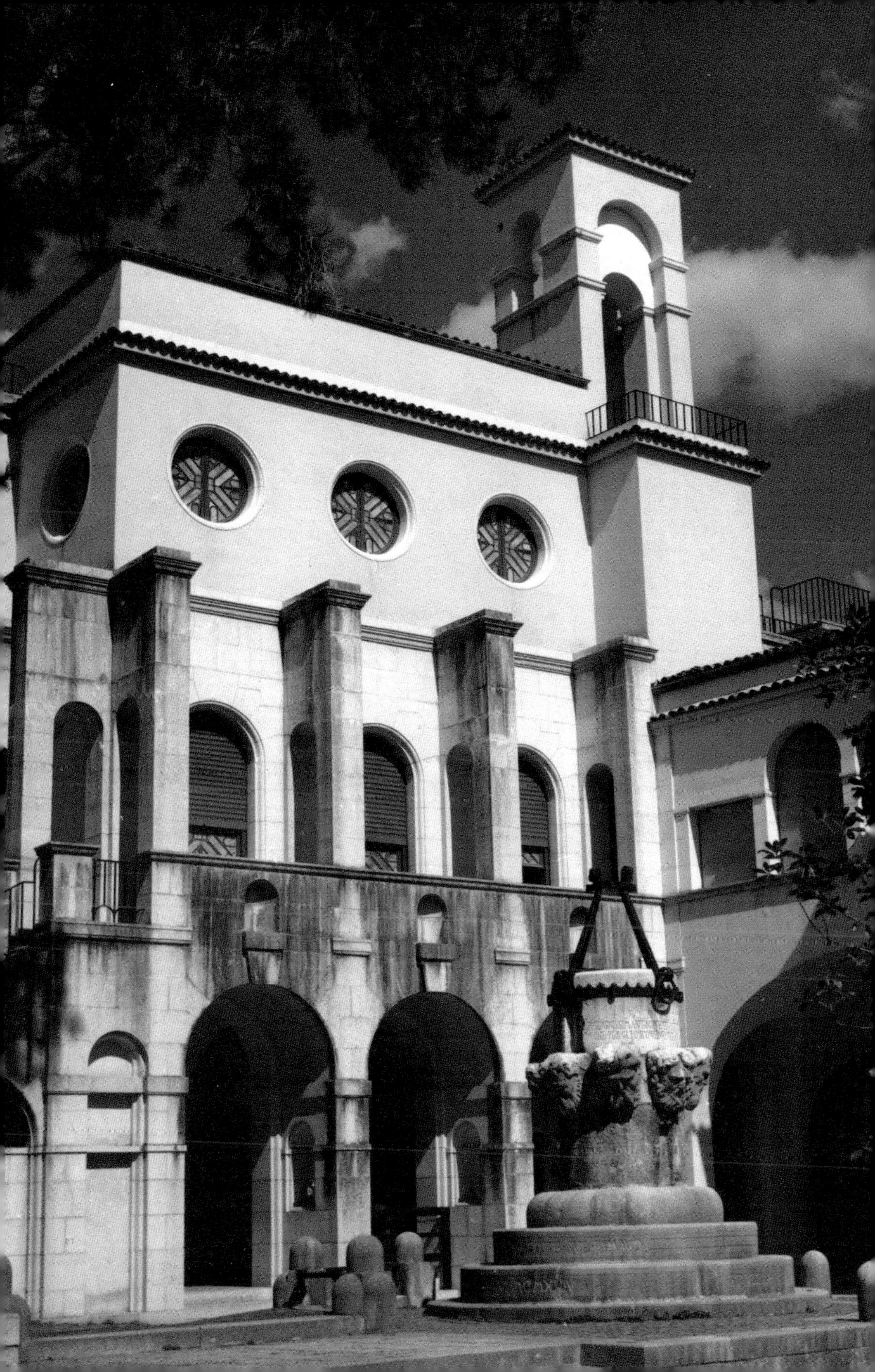

Display case of the "Beffa di Buccari"

Gabriele d'Annunzio and his companions leaving for the "Beffa di Buccari"

Museo della Guerra (War Museum)

Ingresso (Entrance)

The room leading into the museum has a glass case displaying the black overcoat, gloves, cartridge pouch and cap which d'Annunzio wore during the "Beffa di Buccari" (the Bakar mockery). During the night between 10 and 11 February 1918, d'Annunzio sailed out from the port of Venice on board a motor torpedo boat, 96 (MAS), and, together with two other MAS, managed to enter the harbour of Bakar, in Carnaro, with his companions ("there are thirty of us with one destiny and thirty-one with death") he writes in the *Canzone del Quarnaro*; the thirty included Commandant Costanzo Ciano and the Captain of the Corvetta, Luigi Rizzo). Here, "the greatest of enemies that came to mock your ransom", "laughing at any kind of nets or bars", and ready to "dare the unimaginable", torpedoed a freighter leaving jeering messages for the Austrian fleet in three bottles (including the sentences cited above). The famous "Beffa di Buccari" remains one of the most ostentatious of d'Annunzio's war exploits – all of which were distinguished by their originality and by a sort of "poetry" – as a public, political and military man.

Sala delle Pergamene (Hall of the Parchments)

Hanging on the walls and displayed in the glass case in this room are diplomas and awards, including that of the "legionnaire Luisa Baccara". In the same display case, presented in homage to the commandant's companion and musical colleague, is the baton used by Arturo Toscanini in the two concerts he conducted in Fiume, in November 1920.

The bust of d'Annunzio stands on the table, sculpted by Russian-born sculptor Paolo Troubetzkoy, portraitist to the aristocratic elite during the late nineteenth and early twentieth centuries.

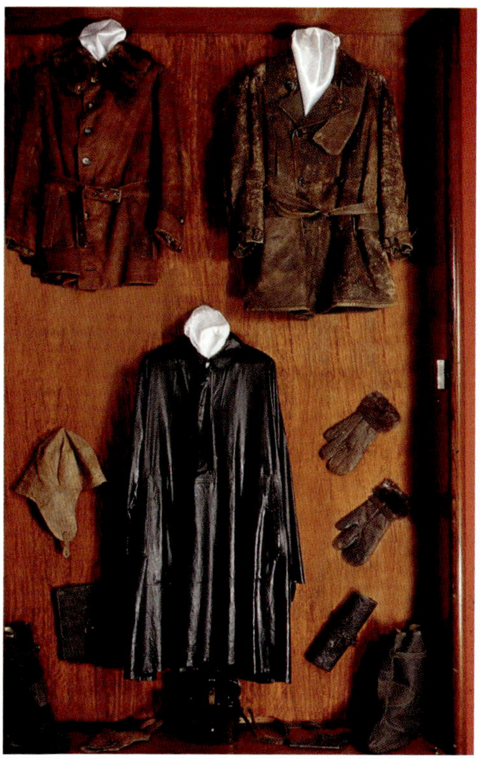

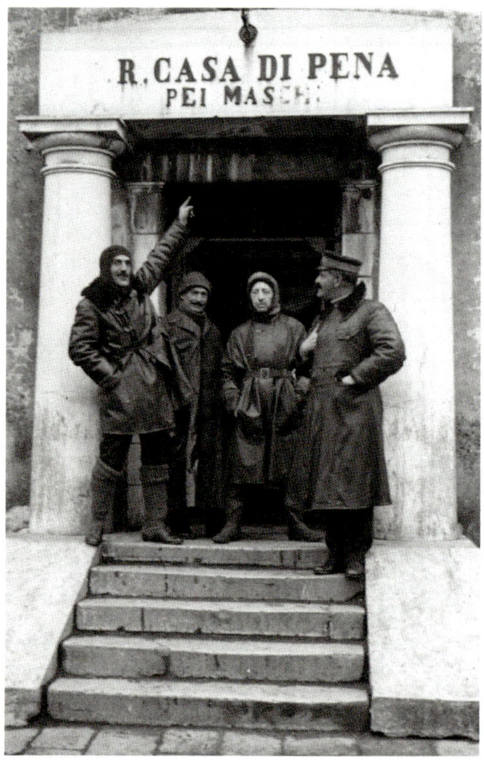

The Shrine of
the Flags

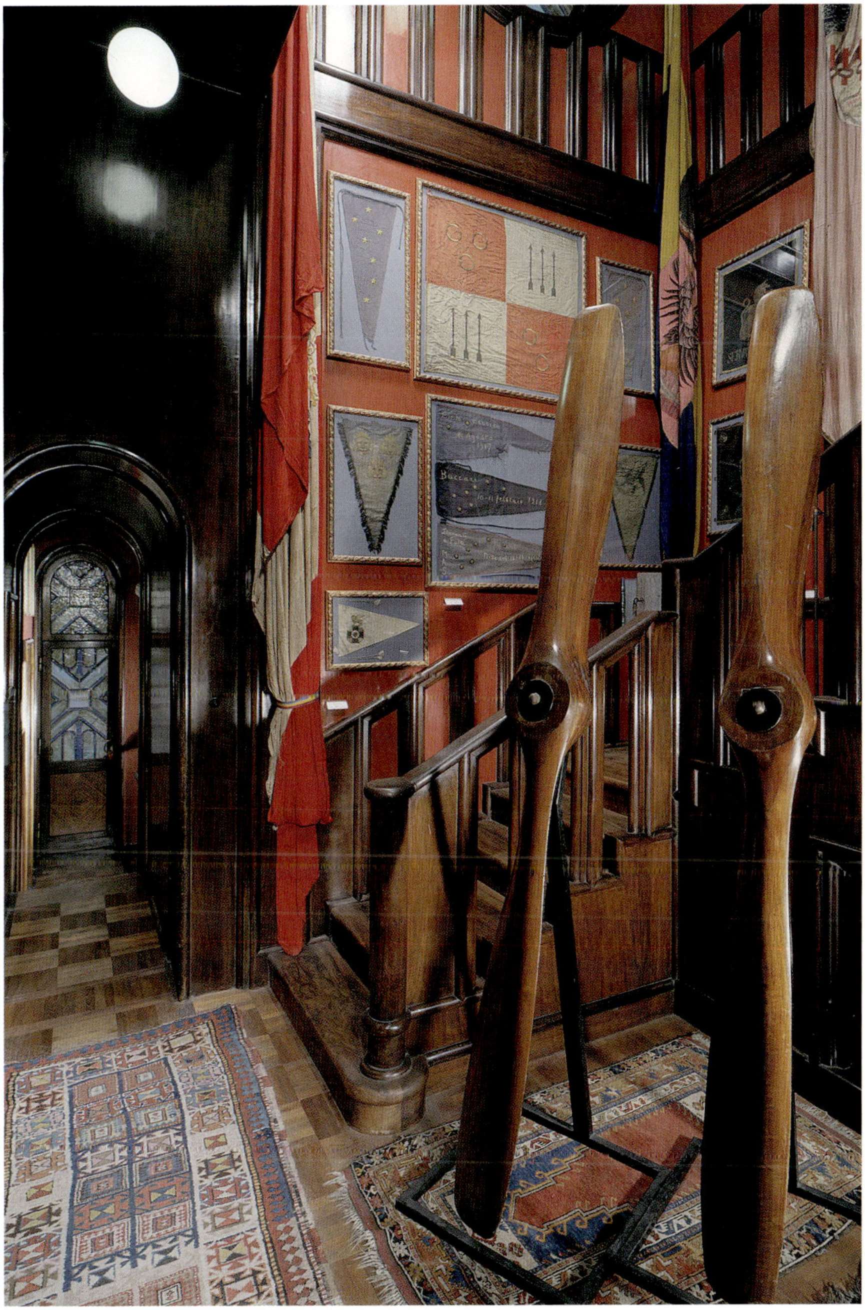

Study

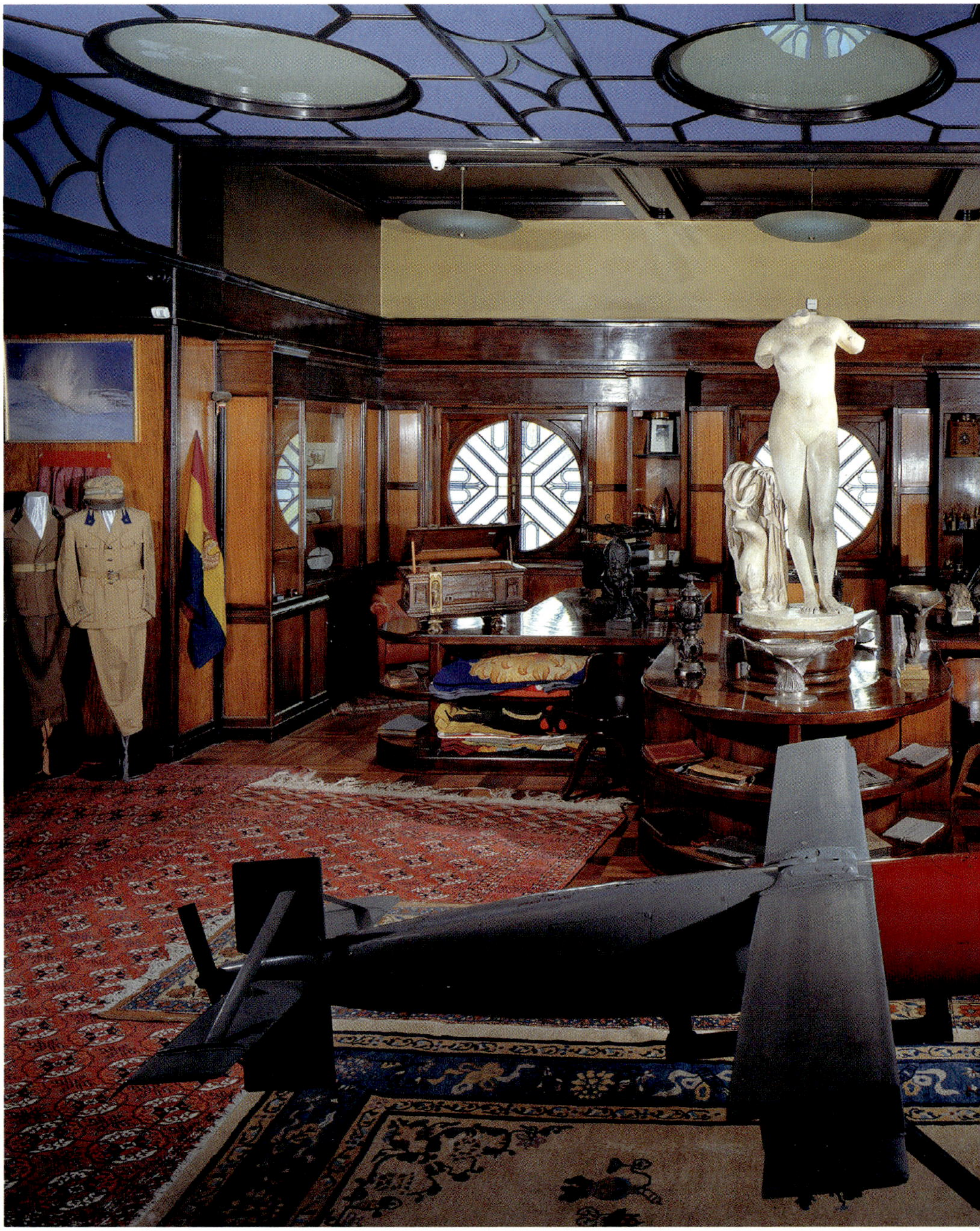

Adolfo Wildt,
The Idiot,
circa 1910

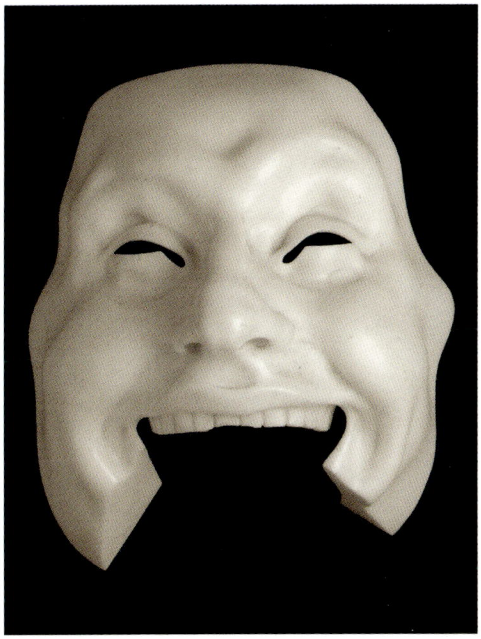

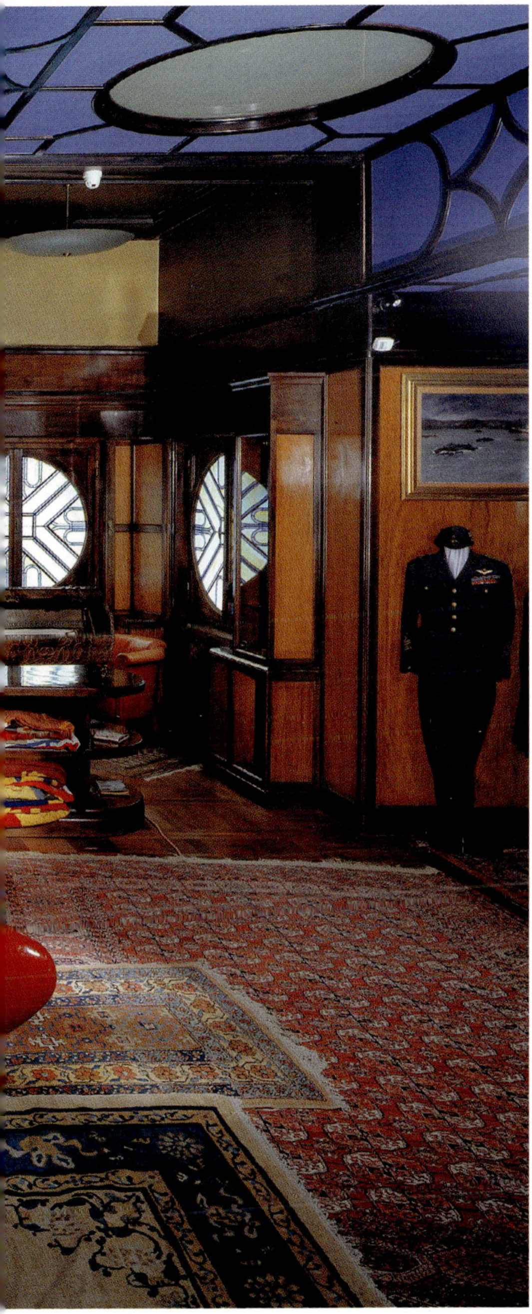

Corridoio (Corridor)

At the end of the corridor are three gas masks, an Austrian ship's bell and a "parlograph", used by d'Annunzio to record his own voice.

Vano scale (Stair well)

Here, in the *Sacrario delle bandiere* (Shrine of the Flags), in addition to the numerous pennants linked to the Fiume exploit (with "I don't give a damn" on one of the mottos), there is the large flag with the coat of arms of the principality of Monte Nevoso, the Gonfalon of the Italian Regency of Carnaro, and the bloodied tricolour flag used to wrap the body of Major Giovanni Randaccio of the 77th Infantry regiment, winner of the gold medal for military valour, who died in d'Annunzio's arms during the battle of the Timavo; the flag was to become a symbol during the Fiume undertaking.
Before continuing up the stairs, there are two propellers from Caproni aeroplanes and an Austrian water-cooled machine gun, seized by a detachment of riflemen during an operation and later given to the poet.

Room of the plaster casts

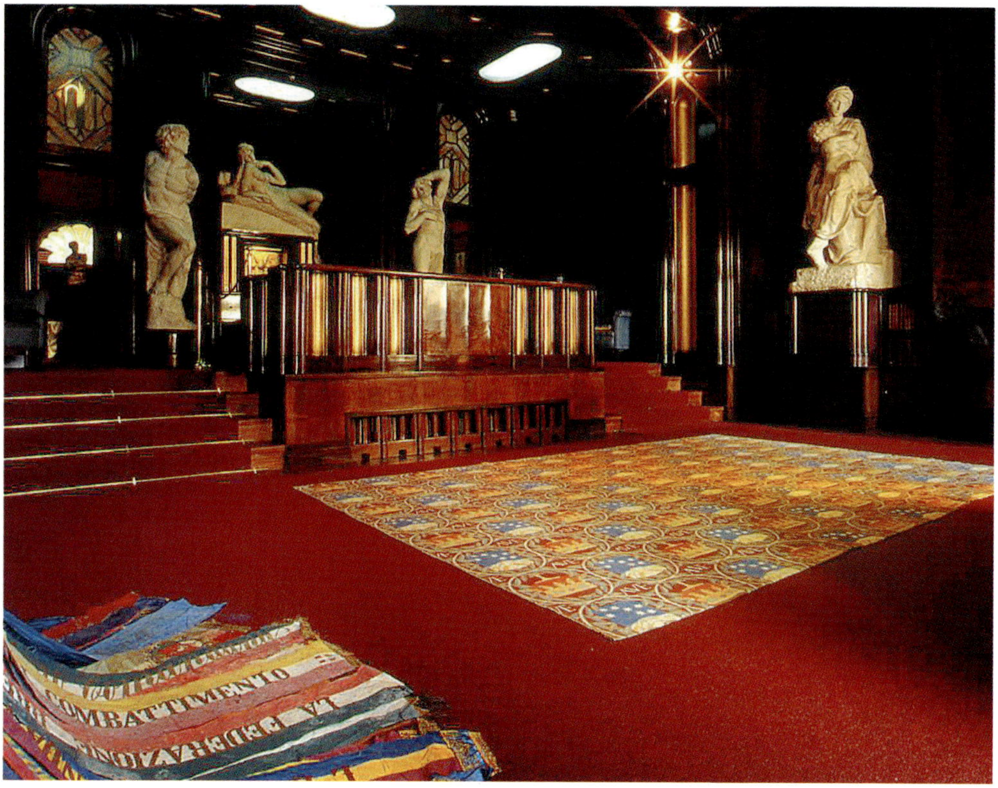

Corridoio del Volo su Vienna (Corridor of the Flight over Vienna)

In the niche are the overcoat, gloves, cap and goggles used by d'Annunzio during the flight over Vienna.

Sala del Camino (Room of the Fireplace)

In the fireplace area, medals, shells, and strips of flag are displayed in eighteenth century reliquaries, in commemoration of the "martyrdom" of the war heroes. The dual control of the twin-engined Caproni plane was given to d'Annunzio in 1938 by Filippo Tommaso Marinetti, futurist and now "aero-poet".

Studio (Study)

In what d'Annunzio intended to be the "new workshop", designed in every small detail by Maroni, everything is in the form of a ship's deck: the porthole-like windows, the alabaster stained glass, the wood panelling, and the large desk in the shape of the ship's bridge. Mixed in with the war "relics" and private relics – uniforms, flags, medals, bayonets and firearms, and, dominating from the centre of the room, the "Crocco", a prototype 1926 bomber – are works of art of the greatest quality, including the rare marble sculpture of *The Idiot* by Milanese sculptor Adolfo Wildt, made in about 1910.

The great portrait of d'Annunzio in aviator uniform is a work by the beautiful, ambiguous American painter Romaine Brooks, who had a relationship with Gabriele (she was also the lover of Ida Rubinstein); d'Annunzio called her "Cinerina" (ash grey) because of the dominant grey colour of her paintings. The stained glass in the small bathroom is by Gio Ponti.

Ojetti describes the study on a visit in August 1937: "The new study and the poet's new bedrooms have sol-

Gaetano Previati,
Nocturne, 1908

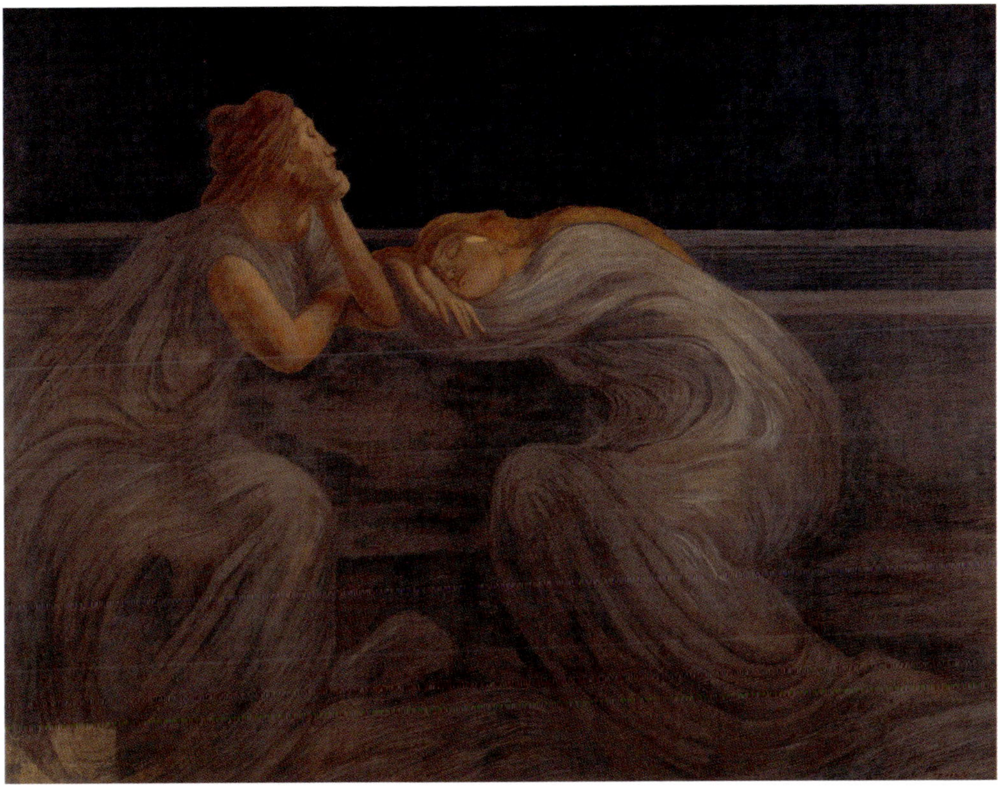

id furniture, all in shiny walnut, broad and indestructible, starting with the writing desk which has the large surface flanked on either side by two equally large tables: the shutters are hermetically sealed to provide the solitude of night when he wishes, even in the middle of the day in summer […]."

Sala dei Calchi o dell'Aurora
(Room of the Plaster Casts or of Aurora)

"In the bedroom, three plaster casts by Michelangelo watch over the bed [...]," Ojetti's description continues. The new bedroom (which Gabriele never actually slept in), also called the "Stanza dell'Aurora", houses casts – of two *Prisoners*, the *Madonna with Child* and the *Aurora* – by Michelangelo, one of d'Annunzio's favourite artists. These provide a solemn presence in the room which is furnished, like all the other rooms in this new area, with solemn twentieth century grandeur: opaline ceiling lighting, alabaster stained glass by Pietro Chiesa, a gilded coffered ceiling, designed by Maroni and made by the Brescia cabinet-maker Ettore Canali – who planned all the furniture in Schifamondo together with Maroni – and dark wood panelling with gilded niches and lacquered surfaces. Above the bed is a large *Winged and Seeing Eye*, in gold, designed by Renato Brozzi: written on a scroll is the motto "in order not to sleep, in order not to die". Previously used as the motto of the Florentine Marchesi Bartolini-Salimbeni, d'Annunzio made it his own, written in red and surrounded by laurel leaves and berries, from the time of his stay in the villa La Capponcina in Settignano. Reproduced in Murano glass, ornamenting doors and windows, engraved on architraves, friezes, stones and majolica, and printed on the poet's letter paper, it was intended as a constant spur to work and

Room of the plaster casts

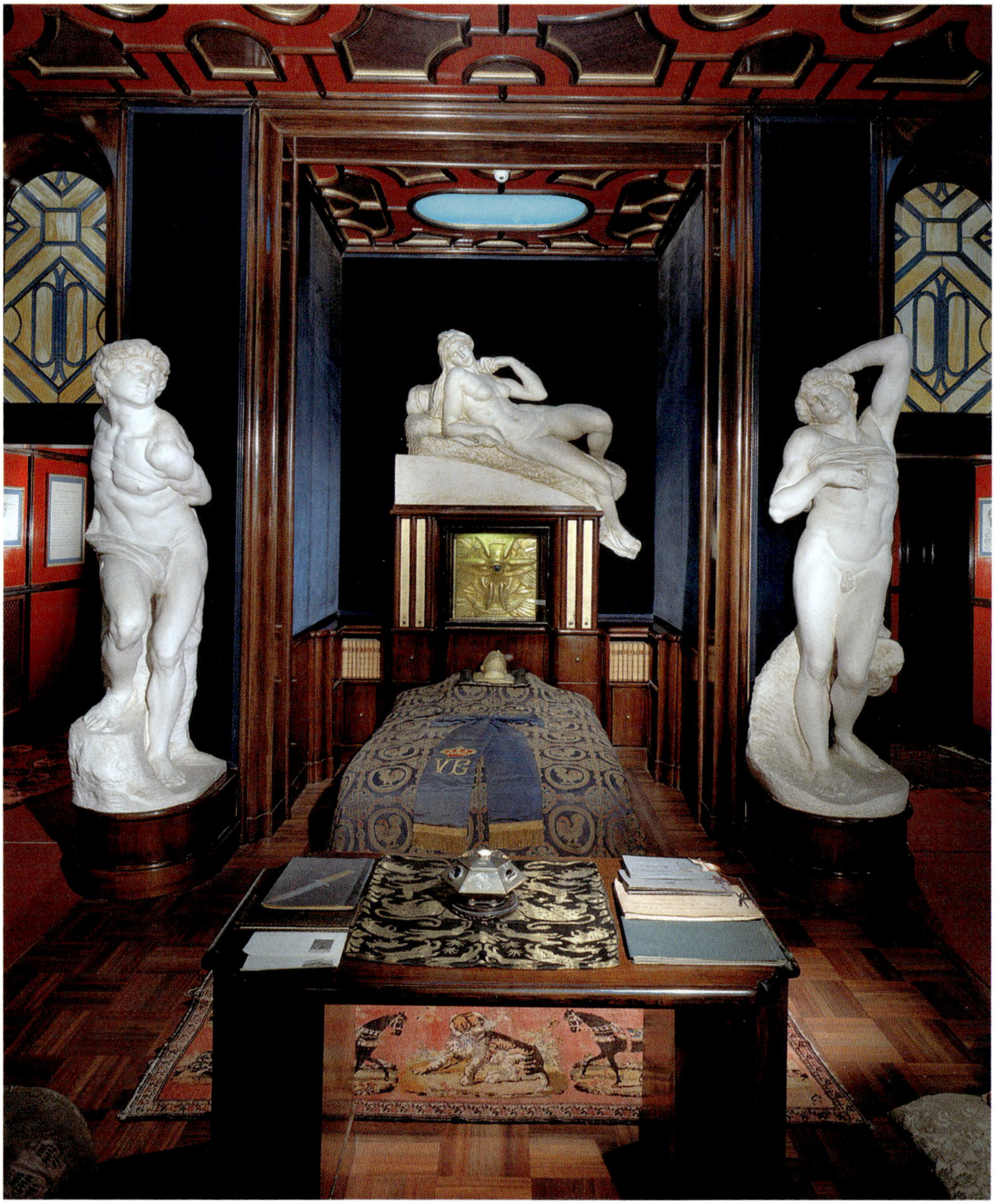

creativity. The walls are decorated with five allegorical panels by the Divisionist painter Gaetano Previati, depicting *Harmony*, *Dance*, *Nocturne*, the *Wind* and a group of *Putti* (Cherubs). This cycle of oil paintings was intended for the music room in the Milan residence of the art dealer Alberto Grubicy. Painted in 1908, and presented at the Salon d'Automne in Paris in 1909 and, in part (only two of them), but with enormous success, at the Venice Biennale in 1912, the paintings were donated to d'Annunzio by Grubicy; after a tortuous sequence of events, finally arrived at the Vittoriale in 1958.
The bed, covered with a fine antique "cockerel bedspread", was where Gabriele's body was laid out on 2 March 1938; his solemn funeral was attended by citizens and authorities, chief among them Benito Mussolini. The marble death mask, made by Arrigo Minerbi, now rests on the pillow.

Sala della Venere (Venus Room)

The room takes its name from the gilded plaster cast of the *Venus of Milo*, the perfectly proportioned image of feminine beauty according to the canons of the classical world and houses two columns and an ancient capital, two sub-machine guns, the base of the machine gun turret from a Caproni aeroplane and the engine of the SVA 10 biplane from the flight over Vienna. On the walls are photographs of the chapel of rest set up inside the control room of the *Puglia* in November 1929, for the funeral of Guido Keller, the most fervent of the Fiumi legionnaires and an eccentric, inventive character.

Corridoio and Sala del Cristo (Corridor and Christ Room)

Hanging in the corridor is a photographic portrait of Francesco Baracca, nicknamed the "Ace of the Aces", Commandant of the 91st Ace Squadron, shot down in June 1918 on Montello, near Padua. At the end of the corridor there are two display cases containing the cloth balaclava helmets which d'Annunzio used in his aeroplanes and on the MAS. Photographs and documents are also displayed in the Sala del Cristo.

Sala dei Ritratti (Portraits Room)

This room has a collection of portraits of d'Annunzio, and the wooden models made by Maroni for the Mausoleum, the hangar for the MAS and the tomb realized for Luisa d'Annunzio in the cathedral of Pescara.

Paolo Troubetzkoy,
Portrait of Gabriele d'Annunzio,
circa 1892

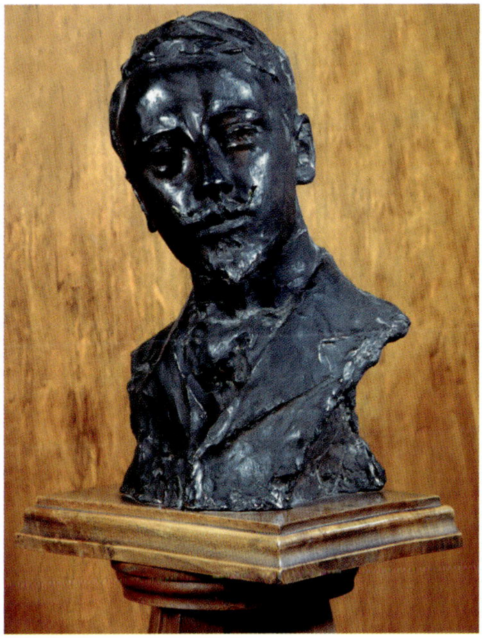

Auditorium

Hanging from the dome of this large hall is the two-seater bomber and reconnaissance biplane (SVA 10) in which d'Annunzio took off for Vienna from the Campo di San Pelagio near Treviso, on 9 August 1918; the plane was piloted by Commandant Natale Palli. The 87th Squadron, known as "La Serenissima", (made up of eleven Ansaldo SVA surveillance aircraft, although four of the planes were forced to turn back), carrying out the plan devised by d'Annunzio in 1917, flew over the capital of the Austro-Hungarian capital at a height of 800 metres and dropped 50,000 leaflets in Italian, exalting "with bold joy" and "to prove what we dare to do", the "wind of victory arising from the rivers of liberty". 350,000 copies of another text were also dropped, written by Ugo Ojetti and translated into German, which was less lyrical but equally clear in its message to the Austro-Hungarian government, "the enemy of national liberty".

Auditorium,
the SVA 10
two-seater bomber
and reconnaissance
biplane

D'Annunzio and
Commandant Natale
Palli on the SVA used
for the flight over
Vienna on 9 August
1918

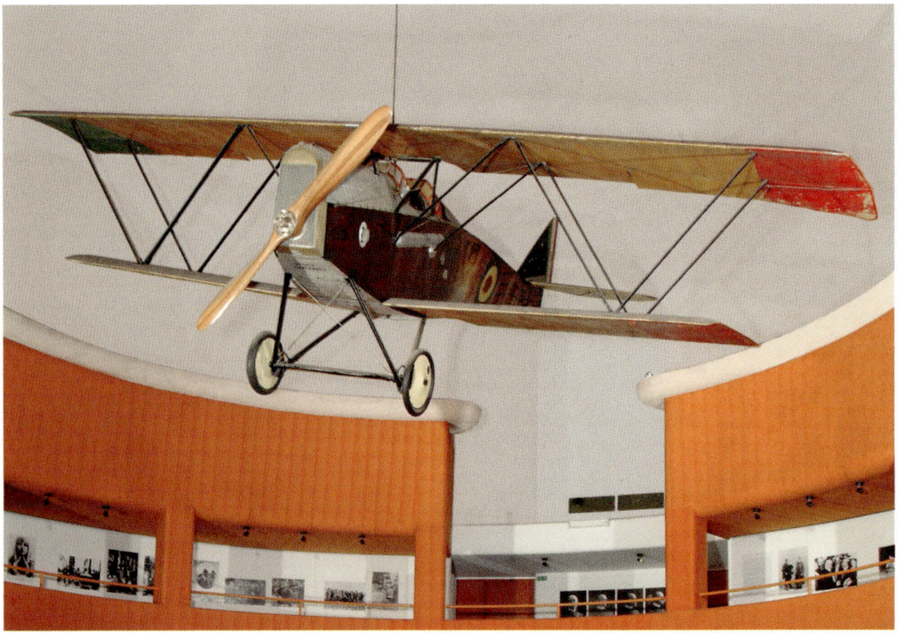

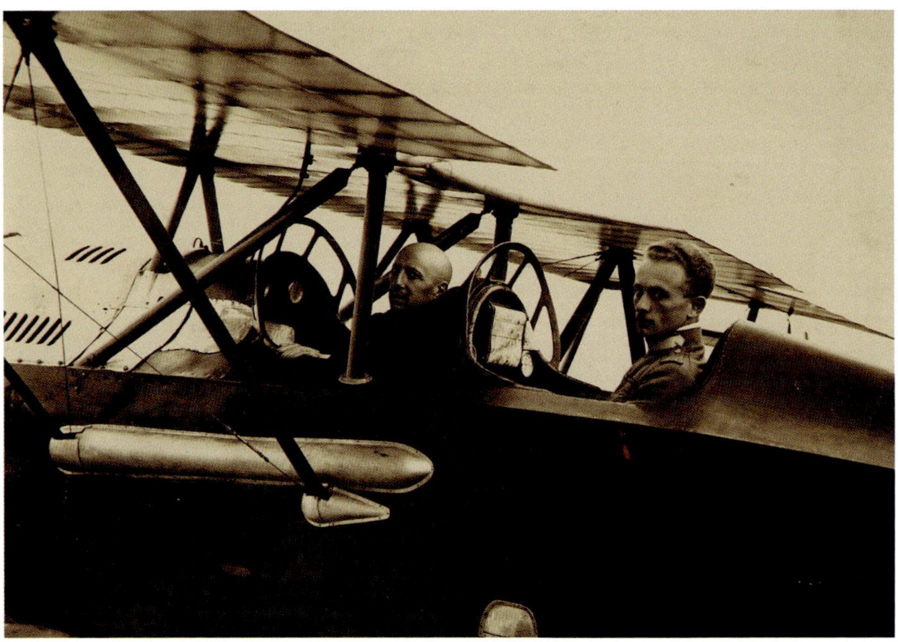

Gabriele d'Annunzio and the 87th "Serenissima" Squadron leaving for the flight over Vienna

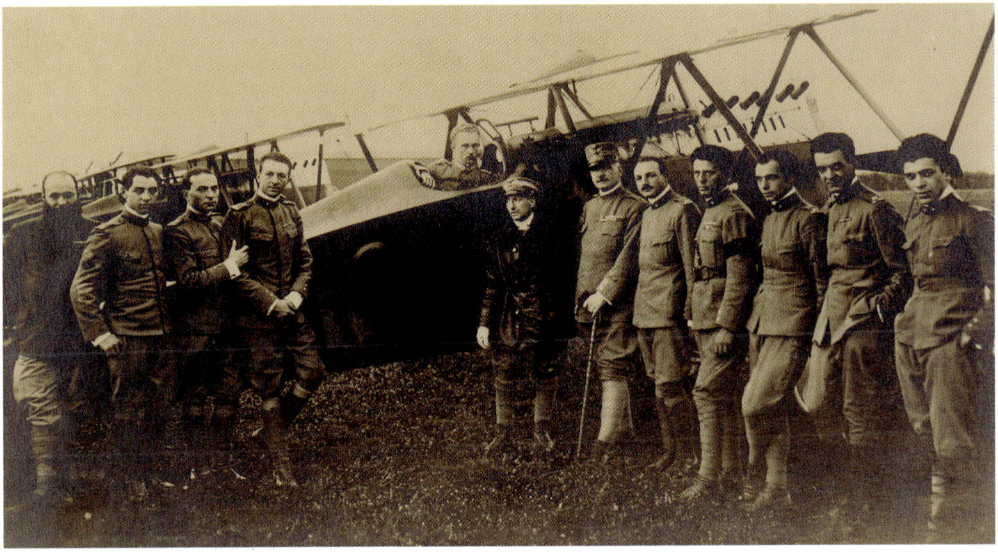

A few hours later, the squadron was on its way home. To commemorate the exploit, d'Annunzio decided to have the seven stars of the Great Bear constellation represented on the gonfalon of the Regency of Carnaro and on the coat of arms of the Principality of Monte Nevoso, seven for the number of aeroplanes that reached Vienna. The effects of the exploit on public opinion in Vienna, Italy and the world were enormous and d'Annunzio was nominated for the Gold Medal for military valour.

Almost every day, as we know from the many "programme notes" that have been preserved, d'Annunzio delighted himself and his guests with a film projection: "We will have music and vision," he wrote, inviting his friend Caterina Ercoliani Cervis to a film evening. Italian cinema, with great classics of the cinema of the Twenties, such as *Scipione l'Africano* (which won the Mussolini cup for best Italian film at the Venice Film Festival in 1937, starring one of the divas of the time, the beautiful Isa Miranda, and with Alberto Sordi making his debut); German avant-garde cinema (*Metropolis* and *Siegfried* by Fritz Lang); American cinema, with the Cecil B. De Mille epics, the Charlie Chaplin films (The *Gold Rush*), the Laurel and Hardy comedies (much loved in Italy as Stanlio and Ollio), and adventure films and comedies with stars of the era such as Errol Flynn and Olivia de Havilland (*The Charge of the Light Brigade*), Jean Harlow and Spencer Tracy (*Libeled Lady*), and finally Westerns and cartoons.

In accordance with d'Annunzio's wishes, the hall still holds concerts, exhibitions and conferences.

Parco (Park)

The Viale di Aligi, named after the heroine of *Figlia di Iorio*, d'Annunzio's successful drama of 1903 which was staged in the gardens of the Vittoriale in 1927 with scenery designed by Maroni, leads from Schifamondo up to the Mausoleum, d'Annunzio's funeral monument constructed by Maroni after the death of his beloved "commandant". In front, the fountain of the dolphin collects the water from the Acqua Pazza stream, one of the two mountain streams (the other is the Acqua Savia – Wise water) into which Maroni divided the Torto stream, the original small water course at the Vittoriale. The gentle trickling of the water cheered d'Annunzio – he had very sensitive hearing – during his residence in the Prioria.

Continuing up, you come to the MAS 96 from the "Beffa di Buccari" (Mockery of Bakar). The MAS

Lake of Dances

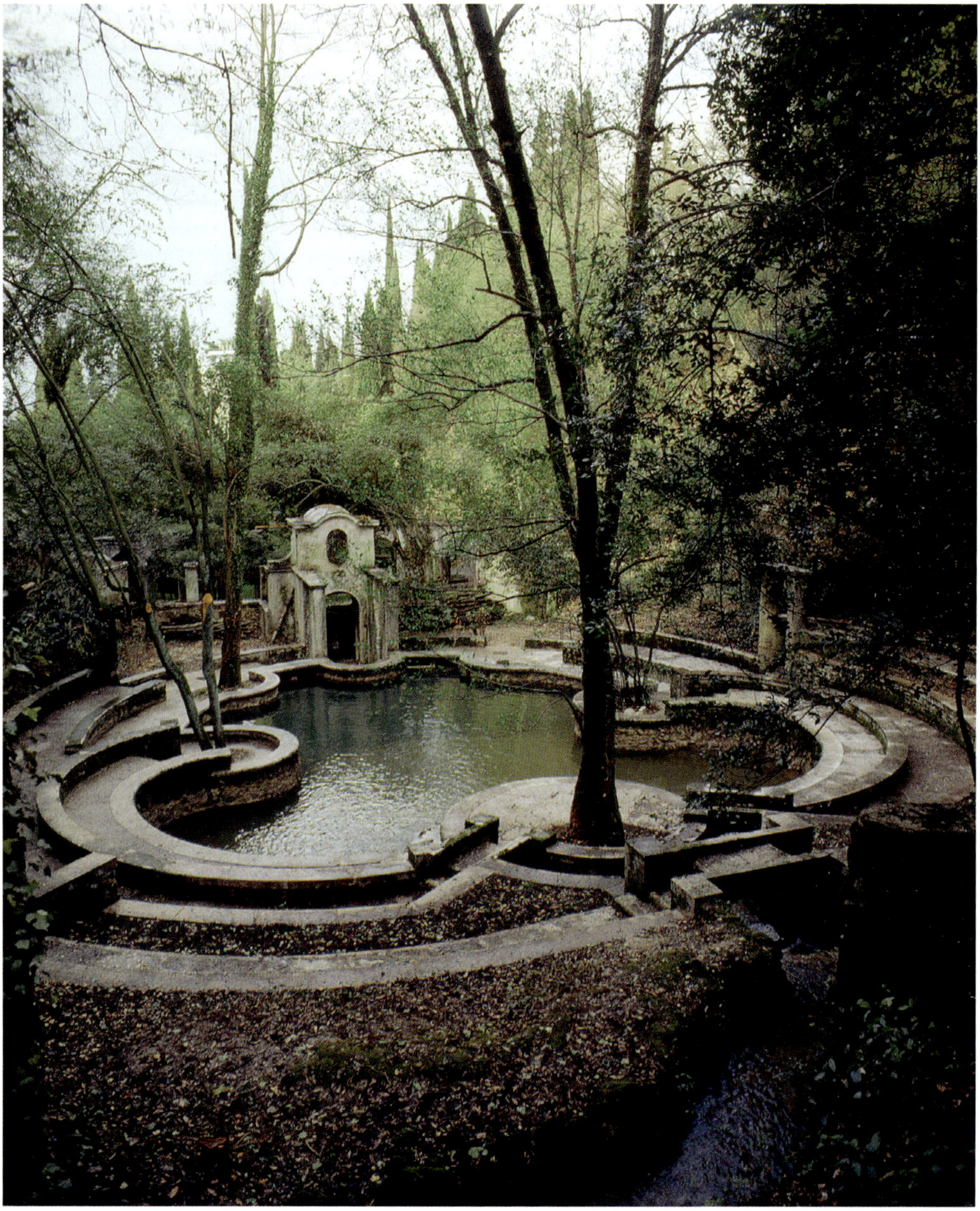

Plinio Codognato,
Riunione motonautica internazionale. Coppa d'Annunzio per la rapidità pura, 1930

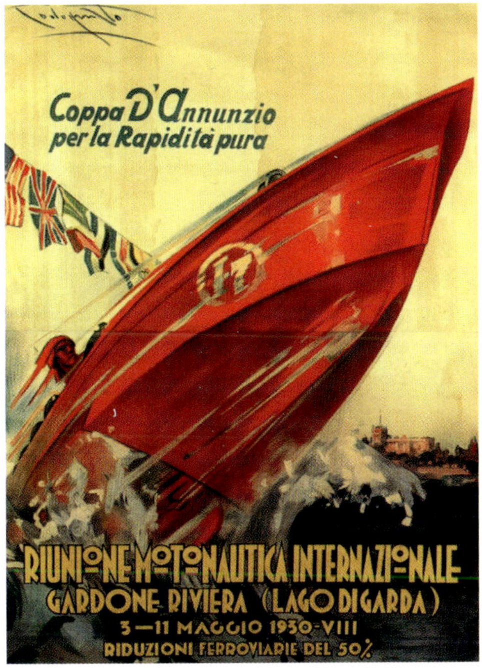

(which stands for *motoscafo-anti-sommergibile*, or anti-submarine motorboat, to which Gabriele added the motto "memento audere semper" (Remember to dare always) arrived at the Vittoriale in January 1923 as a gift from the Council of Ministers through the Minister for the Navy, Admiral Paolo Thaon di Revel; at that time it was berthed on the lake, in the dock constructed by Maroni at the neo-Gothic tower, bought in 1925 (Torre Ruhland was re-named Torre San Marco by the poet). D'Annunzio, who never omitted the smallest detail, gave precise directions for the painting of the boat: the colour was to be "deep blue, the colour of a clear sky". Gabriele used the MAS to go on trips and have races on Lake Garda. He was a Futurist before the Futurists, in fact, and had always loved speed, machines, and flying; he had been an "aviator poet" during the First World War – just as Filippo Tommaso Marinetti would become an "aero-poet" and promoted and participated in sporting activities that took place on and around the waters of the lake, which seemed to him like a "gentle ocean". In 1925 he succeeded in getting Mussolini to agree to build a road around the lake to link it with west bank (christened the *Meandro del Benaco*), and he would drive along it in his sports cars, two *Isotta Fraschini*, one yellow and white, and one blue, which are still preserved under the Esedra porticos. He sponsored boating competitions, and flew over the lake himself on the S 16 Ter seaplane, named *Alcyone* after one of his most famous collections of poetry.

The prow of the cruiser Puglia arrived at the Vittoriale at the same time as the MAS; this was the boat that, together with 504 other ships, had protected the Serbian army from the Austro-Hungarian army between December 1915 and February 1916. Having been dismantled and transported in twenty railway wagons, it was reassembled between 1925 and 1938, when the stone reconstruction of the stern was completed. The new Puglia, a kind of enormous secular reliquary, with the large bronze statue of the *Victory of the Piave* (1932) by sculptor Renato Brozzi, was put into place, once the scenery used for staging a scene from *Figlia di Iorio* had been demolished, on a "plateau that juts out in the form of a prow" towards the lake and the Adriatic, as d'Annunzio wrote to Thaon di Revel. The second mast houses the "Tempietto" (Little temple), dedicated to those who died at sea, while from 2002 onwards, the interior has been used to display models of ships owned by Duke Amedeo d'Aosta.

Below the "plateau", the two streams, Acqua Pazza and Acqua Savia, flow into the "Laghetto delle Danze" (Lake of Dances) in the shape of a violin, which according to the original plans, was to be used to hold dance performances on the central stage. The bridge has iron heads topped with large shells which were given to d'Annunzio by General Armando Diaz, commander-in-chief of the Royal army during the first World War (replacing Luigi Cadorna who was dismissed following the defeat at Caporetto), who was named the Duke of Victory at the end of the war.

Gabriele d'Annunzio and Benito Mussolini on the MAS

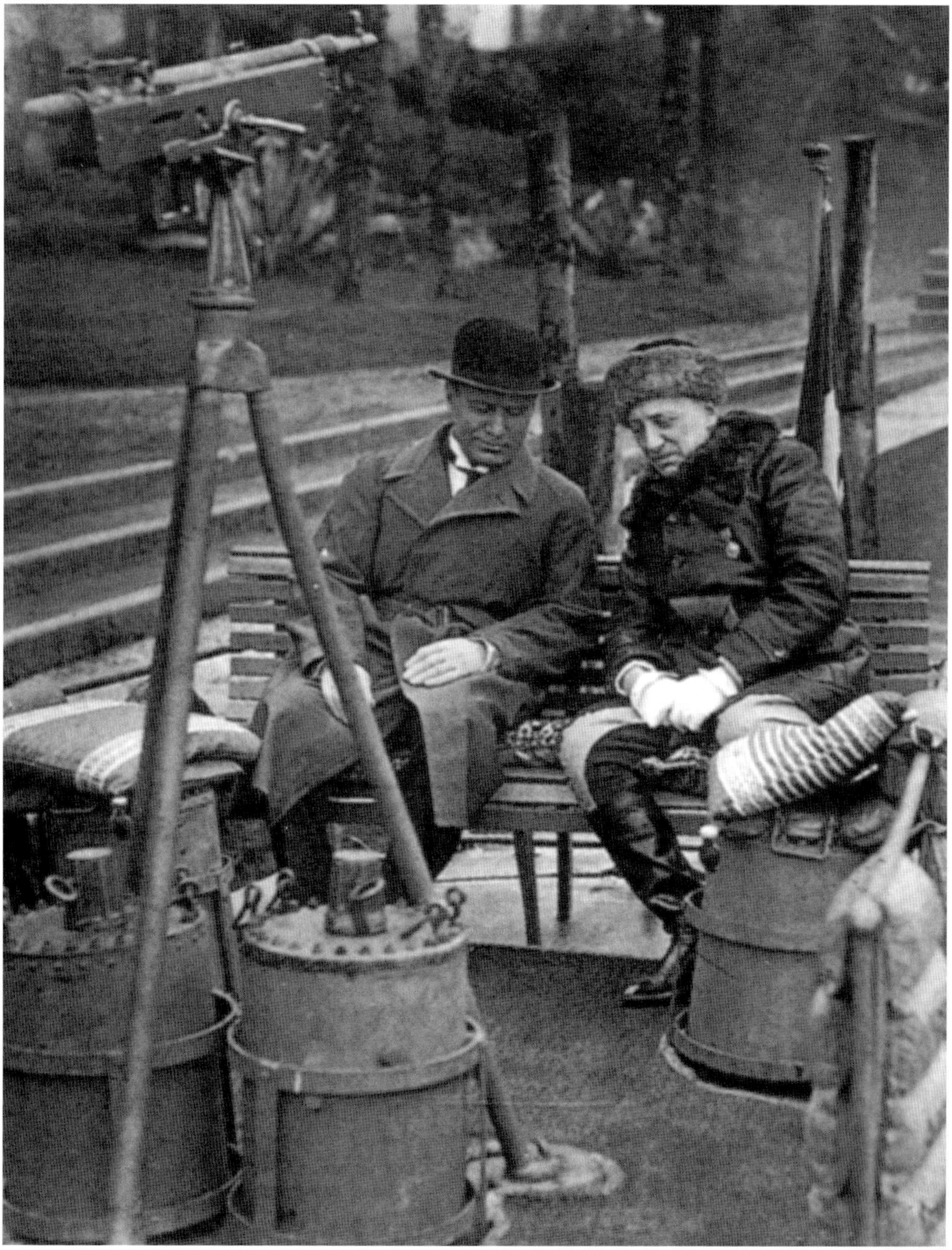

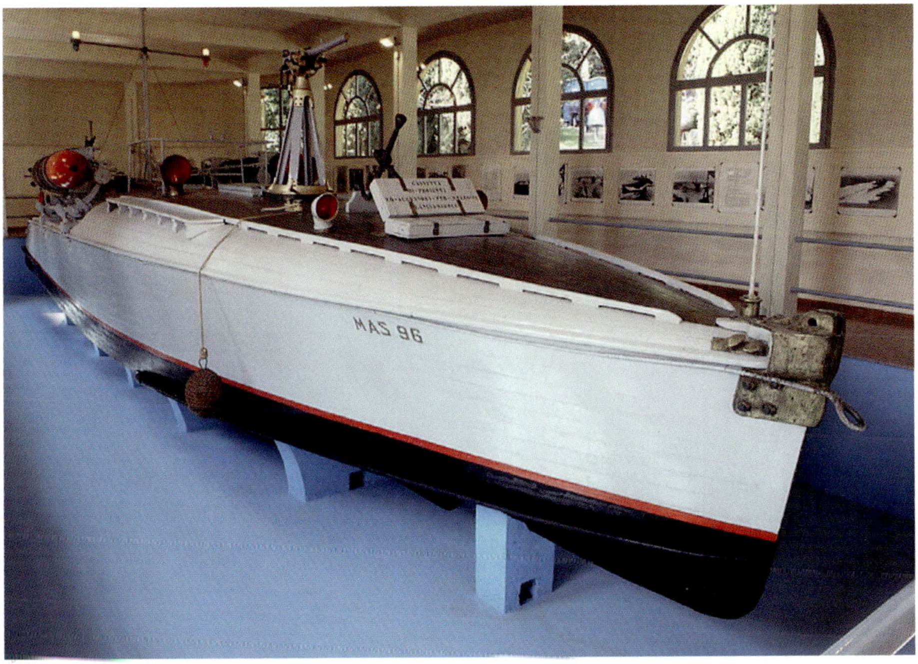

MAS

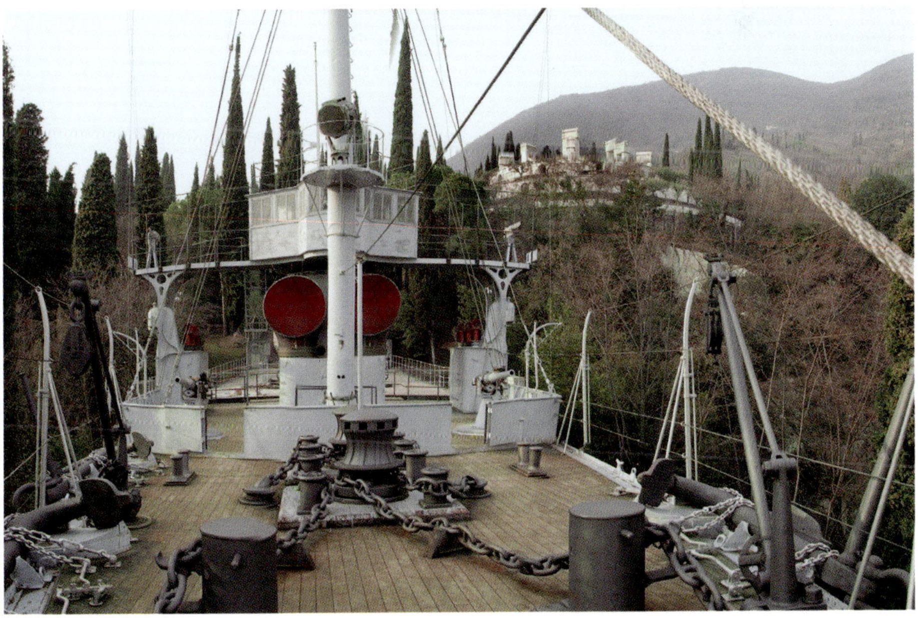

The cruiser *Puglia* with the Mausoleum in the background

Renato Brozzi,
angular Victory for
the prow of the
cruiser Puglia

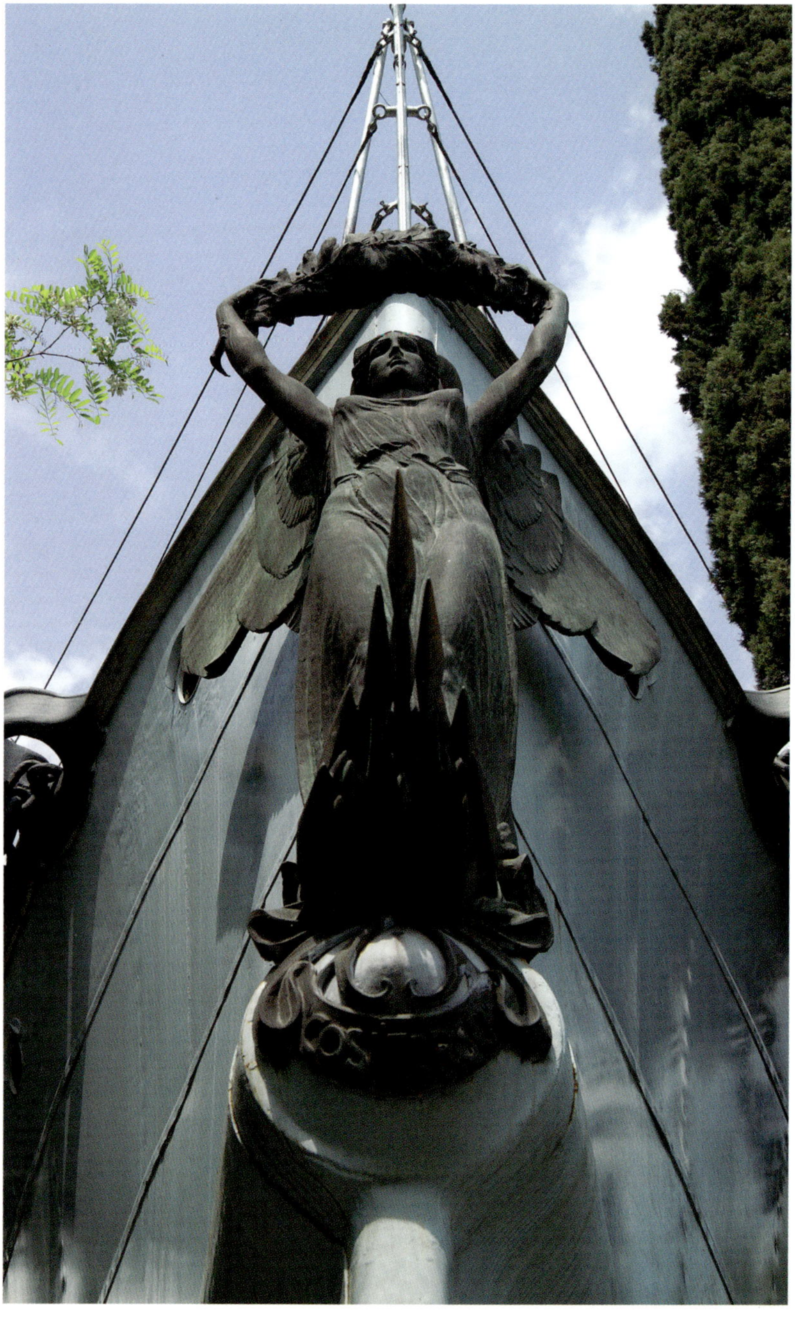

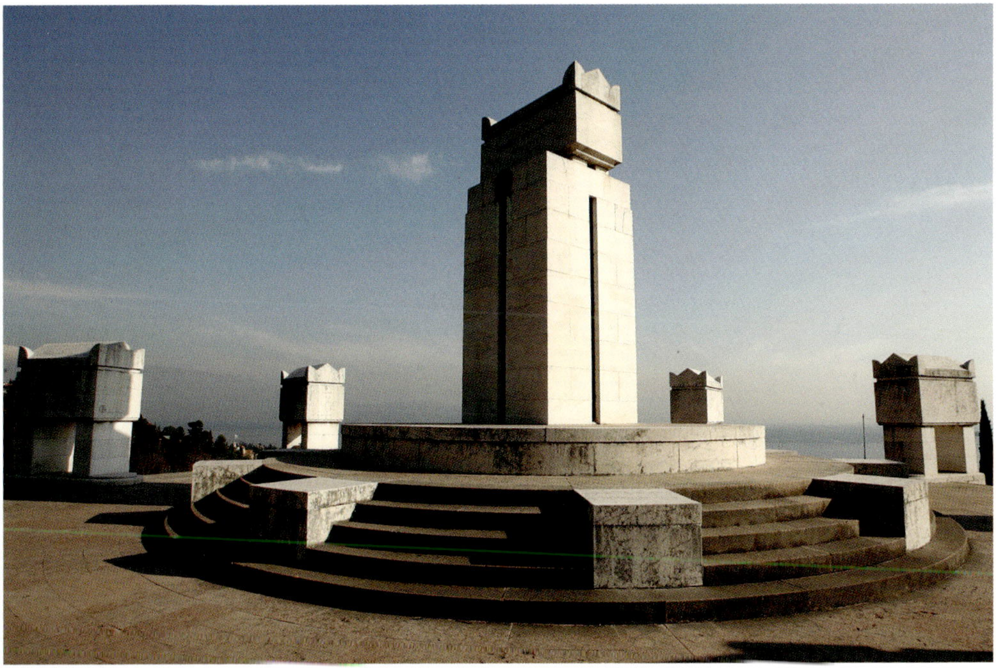

Mausoleo (Mausoleum)

At the highest point of the Vittoriale, a triple ring of walls – the Walls of the Victory of the Humble, of the Sappers, and of the Heroes – surrounds the Mausoleum, which has echoes of ancient burial places, starting with its circular shape. Ten sarcophagi, housing the remains of nine of the Fiume legionnaires, including Guido Keller and Gian Carlo Maroni, are arranged in a circle, standing guard over the tomb containing d'Annunzio's remains (since 1963, the centenary of his birth), which is elevated so that it dominates the whole area.

Inside the Mausoleum is a rock from Adamello (in the Alps, one of the most important strategic fronts in the First World War) and a large crucifix by the symbolist sculptor Leonardo Bistolfi.

The construction is very impressive and Gabriele gave a lot of meditiations to it: "For my internal perfection it is necessary for me to have my tomb raised on four columns, and for me to be able to go and visit it every day," he wrote to Renato Brozzi in 1930, proving yet again how every detail inside the Vittoriale was designed to perpetuate the glory of its owner, of his deeds of art and war, of his works, and of his whole existence. Indeed, the poet wrote in a note dated 25 March 1930: "Superior to poetry, philosophy, or politics is the supreme art of living. Solus scis vivere."

Bibliography

There is a huge bibliography of the life and works of Gabriele d'Annunzio. We have chosen to include only a few titles of books quoted from or referred to in this book, as well as some other publications that may be useful in providing further information about the Vittoriale.

A tavola con D'Annunzio, P. Sorge (edited by), Electa, Milan 1998

Album D'Annunzio, with a biographical-critical essay and commentary on the illustrations A. Andreoli; iconographic research by E. Romano, A. Mondadori, Milano 1990

A. Andreoli, *Il vivere inimitabile. Vita di Gabriele d'Annunzio*, Mondadori, Milan 2000

A. Andreoli, *Il Vittoriale degli Italiani*, Skira, Milan 2004

T. Antongini, *Vita segreta di d'Annunzio*, Mondadori, Milan 1938

D'Annunzio e la promozione delle arti, catalogue of the exhibition (Gardone Riviera), R. Bossaglia and M. Quesada (edited by), Mondadori-De Luca, Milan-Rome 1988

G. d'Annunzio, *Di me a me stesso*, A. Andreoli (edited by), Mondadori, Milan 1990

G. d'Annunzio, *Le cento e cento e cento e cento pagine del Libro segreto di Gabriele d'Annunzio tentato di morire* (1935), P. Gibellini (edited by), Mondadori, Milan 1995

G. d'Annunzio, *Siamo spiriti azzurri e stelle. Diario inedito (17-27 agosto 1922)*, P. Gibellini (edited by), Giunti, Florence 1995

D'Annunzio innovatore, catalogue of the exhibition (Milan), A. Andreoli (edited by), Biblioteca di via Senato, Milan 2000

G. d'Annunzio, *Il befano alla befana. L'epistolario con Luisa Baccara*, P. Sorge (edited by), Garzanti, Milan 2003

F. Di Tizio, *La Santa Fabbrica del Vittoriale nel carteggio inedito D'Annunzio - Maroni*, Ianieri, Pescara 2009

G. Gatti, *Le donne nella vita e nell'arte di Gabriele d' Annunzio*, Guanda, Modena 1951

Il guardaroba di Gabriele D'Annunzio: conformismo e trasgressione, catalogue of the exhibition (Florence), A. Andreoli (edited by), La Nuova Italia, Scandicci 1988

G.B. Guerri, *D'Annunzio. L'amante guerriero*, Mondadori, Milan 2008

A. Mazza, *D'Annunzio e il Vittoriale. Guida alla casa del poeta*, Edizioni del Vittoriale, Gardone 1985

A. Mazza, *Vittoriale. Casa del sogno di Gabriele d'Annunzio*, Edizioni del Puntografico, Brescia 1988

Il Museo della Guerra di Gabriele d'Annunzio al Vittoriale degli Italiani, A. B. Spada, L. Faverzani (edited by), Grafo, San Zeno Naviglio 2008

U. Ojetti, *Cose Viste*, 2 voll., Sansoni, Florence 1951

Per non dormire: eleganze notturne al Vittoriale, catalogue of the exhibition (Gardone Riviera), P. Sorge (edited by), Electa, Milano 2000

Il piacere del corpo: D'Annunzio e lo sport, catalogue of the exhibition (Gardone Riviera), M. Pancera, G. Vergani (edited by); con la consulenza di V. Pirlo, Electa, Milan 1999

C. Salaris, *Alla festa della rivoluzione. Artisti e libertari con d'Annunzio a Fiume*, Il Mulino, Bologna 2002

P. Sorge, *L'arte della seduzione in Gabriele d'Annunzio*, Carabba, Lanciano 2009

V. Terraroli, *Giancarlo Maroni, Gabriele d'Annunzio e gli artisti per il Vittoriale: un breve itinerario all'interno della "Santa Fabbrica"*, in *L'architetto del lago. Giancarlo Maroni e il Garda*, F. Irace (edited by), Electa, Milan 1993, pp. 125-135.

V. Terraroli, *Il Vittoriale. Percorsi simbolici e collezioni d'arte di Gabriele d'Annunzio*, Skira, Milan 2001

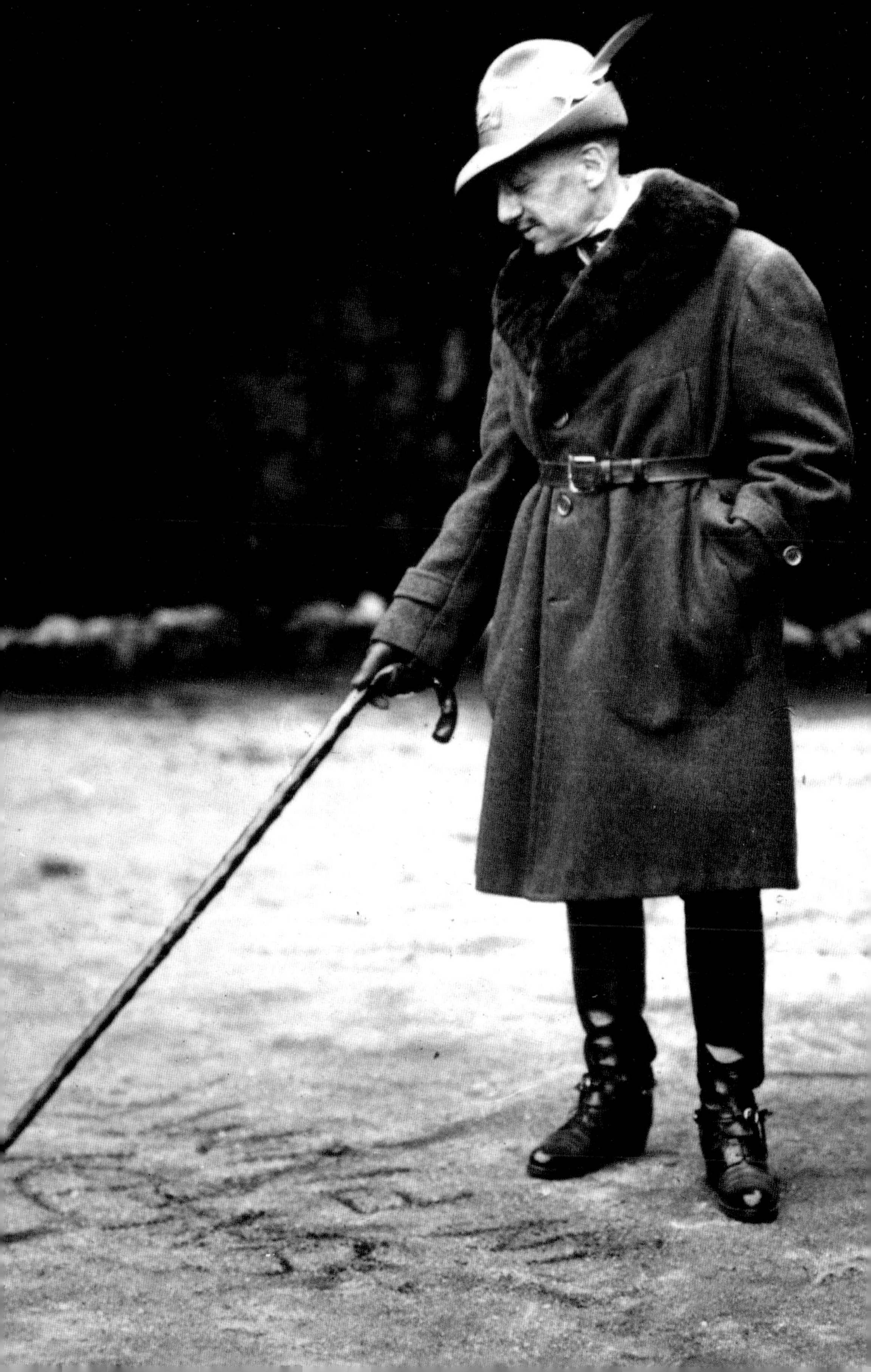

Photo credits:
Archivio Iconografico del Vittoriale.
Rome, Galleria Nazionale d'Arte Moderna.
With the permission of the Ministry for Cultural Heritage.

Silvana Editoriale Spa

via Margherita De Vizzi, 86
20092 Cinisello Balsamo, Milano
tel. 02 61 83 63 37
fax 02 61 72 464
www.silvanaeditoriale.it

Reproduction, printing and binding
by Arti Grafiche Amilcare Pizzi Spa,
Cinisello Balsamo, Milano

Printed
September 2009